The Devil on the Doorstep

My Escape from a Satanic Sex Cult

Annabelle Forest

With Katy Weitz

**SIMON &
SCHUSTER**

London · New York · Sydney · Toronto · New Delhi

A CBS COMPANY

First published in Great Britain by Simon & Schuster UK Ltd, 2014
A CBS COMPANY

Copyright © 2014 by Annabelle Forest and Katy Weitz

1 3 5 7 9 10 8 6 4 2

Simon & Schuster UK Ltd
1st Floor
222 Gray's Inn Road
London WC1X 8HB

www.simonandschuster.co.uk

Simon & Schuster Australia
Sydney

Simon & Schuster India,
New Delhi

A CIP catalogue record for this book is available
from the British Library.

Paperback ISBN: 978-1-47113-668-9
Ebook ISBN: 978-1-47113-669-6

Typeset by Hewer Text UK Ltd, Edinburgh

Printed and bound in Great Britain by CPI Group UK Ltd, Croydon CR0 4YY

The Devil on the Doorstep

Contents

The only thing necessary for the triumph of evil is for good men to do nothing

Edmund Burke

Prologue

Stop. Think. Breathe, I tell myself.

I need to calm down. The tears are stinging my eyes, my heart is going at a million miles an hour and I'm gasping for every breath. Where is she? WHERE IS SHE?

It's 7.30 a.m., a normal school day. Just seconds earlier everything was fine. I'd padded into Emily's room to wake her up, switching on the overhead light then leaving to go to the bathroom. My seven-year-old is such a sleepy head. She always has been. While other parents get woken at ungodly hours of the morning and beg their children for a few minutes extra in bed, Emily has always been a great sleeper. From four months old she slept right through and it's been the same ever since. I'm always up before her. So I like to give her a few minutes to come round before we head into the kitchen for breakfast.

When I return to her bedroom she's still not up, so I lean over her soft, cream duvet to give her a little shake. But instead of touching my sleeping child's shoulder, my hand sinks into the soft feathery cover, right down to the mattress. Shocked, I rip the duvet off the bed. Gone.

In that instant, my whole world shifts. I feel bile start to rise in my throat. I swallow hard. Again and again.

Where is she? Has she been snatched in the night? How long has she been gone?

I feel the blood pounding in my ears now, as I scrabble under the bed. Not there. On all fours, I feel weak, my arms and legs turn to jelly. I want to curl up in a ball and hold myself but I have to find her. Panic now grips my chest and I'm finding it hard to breathe.

Suddenly I hear a familiar little giggle coming from behind the door.

Oh my God. Emily!

I want to scream at her, shake her for putting me through such torture, but I don't. I close my eyes, let my head droop forward and push myself back onto my knees, letting the relief wash over me. I take in a deep, long breath and let it out slowly.

Then, in what I hope passes for a playful voice, I say out loud: 'Now, where has Emily gone this morning?'

More giggles.

'Where on earth can she be? Is she behind the curtain?' I go through the motions of pretending to look for my daughter, playing her game of hide and seek, just like a normal mummy would, all the while knowing full well that she is safe on the other side of the door.

Later, after she has left for school, I cry on my own. It is relief, just relief that she is OK. Are these the reactions of a normal parent?

Am I normal?

I don't know.

It's hard to describe the feelings I have for my daughter, Emily. They are intense beyond belief, beyond reason. I love her so much it hurts. She is my everything – she makes me laugh, makes me smile, makes me angry, happy and hurt. Emily is the reason I feel. She is my entire emotional centre. It's hard to understand my story without knowing her story too, about how she came into this world.

The truth is that I never expected to love Emily. I didn't even want her. Emily was a child of pain – she was born out of coercion, rape and abuse. She was the physical embodiment of all the wrongs that had been done to me from the age of eleven. By the age of eighteen, when I gave birth, I was an empty shell – my life had become meaningless to me. I felt nothing, cared for nobody and wanted no part in this world. That is, until I set eyes on my daughter. In that moment the stone that had set hard around my heart crumbled and I knew at last what love meant. I had someone to live for, someone to love. Emily gave me my life back.

So, you see, my love for my daughter isn't normal. I know that I kiss her and hug her too often; so much that she pushes me away, annoyed at my constant, clamouring affection. I know that I am fiercely protective of her, so much that it isn't healthy for either of us. And I know that those ordinary moments that most parents enjoy – the games of hide and seek, the times when we chase each other through the park or down the aisle of the supermarket – they are not fun for me. They are heart-stopping, agonizing, gut-churning moments of hell. I don't know what I would do if I ever lost Emily. It is my greatest fear.

Of course, one day I will have to tell Emily about her past, about the man who fathered her, Colin Batley. There are things that I would rather not say to her face, things I can barely acknowledge to myself, but I won't be able to protect her from the truth. I won't be able to shield her from her origins and the inevitable pain it will bring. It helps that she looks like me – my almond eyes, my small, puckered mouth, freckled cheeks and button nose. If she resembled him, our lives would be so much harder.

When I look at my daughter and feel my heart swell, it defies all my understanding that there are people like my own mother in this world – a woman capable of harming her own flesh and blood in the way that she harmed me. It makes me think that if she can do that to her own daughter, then anyone can do any-thing to anybody. So I trust no one. At the same time, I know I can't mollycoddle my daughter or hide her from the world. I want her to be strong, capable of standing up to injustice and fighting for herself. She needs to know she can survive without me. So I push her towards the milestones I know she must achieve – even as I mourn the elements of her infancy she leaves behind.

Don't grow up too fast, I whisper under my breath, secretly cherishing the times she still comes running to Mummy. For now, while she is still just a child, she is mine, all mine. And yes, I probably do cuddle her too much, kiss her too often, worry too hard and cry too long. But then, that's a mother's privilege and, once you've read this story, you may understand why I am like that. Why I wake up every day and run into her room, eager to see her face and bask in her love. Why I thank her in my heart for giving me life, for showing me how to love and for bringing me back from hell. Why I never take my eyes off her for a single second. Why I never look away.

This is her story and mine.

Chapter 1

Colin

'Come with me.'

My mother's voice pierced my dreams.

Warm and snug, curled up in a ball under my duvet, I let out a little groan. It felt like I'd only just got into bed but I guess I must have fallen asleep because now it was dark outside and all I could see when I blinked myself awake was my mum's long silhouette framed by the light in the hallway. I was confused. It was night-time still.

'Come on,' she urged impatiently. 'Get up and come with me.'

Reluctantly, I rolled out of bed and let my feet come to rest on the cold wooden floorboards. In the corner, my two-year-old sister Olivia slept soundly in her cot. Mum waited to see I was up, then she turned around and walked down the stairs.

It was July, the height of summer, but this house always felt cold and I shivered in my flimsy yellow and pink flowery night-dress. We'd only just moved to this semi in Wales a few weeks ago from our home in East London but I hated it already. The house was disgusting: dirty brown wallpaper peeled off the walls, there were no carpets, just bare boards or even concrete in places on the floor, and everything was dark and rotten. It was like an old man's house.

Barefoot, I padded down the creaking staircase behind my mum to the living room, which was lit only by a candle on top of the TV in the corner. I squinted towards the back of the room, where I could just make out the figure of a man seated in the dark-purple armchair, tucked into the recess of the wall.

'Come here,' a deep voice commanded.

I walked, reluctantly, towards the man's voice. My mum went to kneel at his side. As I got closer, I could just make out his face in the flickering candlelight – black hair fell long and greasy around his angular cheeks. He had a wide mouth, thin lips and large, square black glasses, and when he spoke I saw he had very few teeth. In fact, it looked like he had only one tooth. The mustard-yellow curtains billowed as a breeze swept into the room – and I shivered.

'Come here, Annabelle,' the man said again.

I didn't want to go any closer. I didn't like the look of this man. He scared me. I just stood there, a few feet away, my hands at my side, as he spoke: 'You know your family has come here to be part of something very special.'

His voice rumbled over me, like a train passing slowly through a station. I was dozy, uncomprehending. All I wanted was to go back to bed, curl up and surrender to sleep. But the man's voice rumbled on: 'This here is where your life in the Church begins. This is going to be a different path for you now, a different path for you, your mother and your sister. And it's important that you learn what is expected of you and what you can do to make your path true to thy own will. We in the Church will try to help you, to guide you in the right way, but it is your path and you have to choose carefully.'

His words barely registered. I swayed slightly, fighting back sleep, as I tried to focus on this man in front of me. Who was he? He seemed very tall because his long, thin limbs appeared to spill out of the chair at every angle. He wore grey tracksuit bottoms, trainers, a football shirt and a black leather jacket. He was talking and talking but nothing made any sense to me.

'The Church will guide you to your path but it is up to you to choose the way to the Palace,' he went on. 'Only you can find your way to the Palace and avoid the eternal pain of the Abyss. The Church will be your life now, and everyone in the Church will be working towards the same end. In order to fulfil your path you must obey the laws of the Church and work towards achieving a way into the Palace. You have a role now, a chance to be something special, to make something of your life . . .'

On and on it went. Once or twice I felt my eyelids shut as he kept talking, but then, at some point, the man made a small gesture with his hand, towards my mum, who was sitting back on her heels, facing him. He moved his other hand towards his crotch and then pulled down the waistband of his tracksuit. Mum edged towards him on her knees and put her head between his legs. Then she started bobbing up and down on his lap. It was dark, and in the flickering candlelight all I could see was the back of her head and her long dark hair draped across her shoulders, as her head moved up and down.

Still, he carried on speaking: 'The Gods are watching over you, Annabelle. They are watching over all of us all of the time.'

What's going on? This is weird and scary.

I wanted to just turn and run out of there, back up to bed, close my eyes and go to sleep.

'Come closer, Annabelle.' He had his hand outstretched towards me now but I didn't want to go to him. I was frozen, rooted to the spot.

This is a bad dream. It can't be real.

'You mustn't be frightened, Annabelle,' he said. 'The only thing to fear in this world is failing to fulfil your own will and failing to reach the Palace. The world is a natural, instinctive place and we must take our place within it. Every man and every woman is a star. Every number is infinite. There is no difference. Come here!'

The instruction was firmer this time. There was something in the way that he spoke, like I didn't have a choice in the matter. I was scared but, slowly, I inched towards him.

'Come forth, oh children of the stars, and take your fill of love!' His voice was louder now. 'Come forth, Annabelle. You are the chosen one. Come forth!'

I didn't know what he meant by any of it but now I was trembling. There was a sharpness to his tone and suddenly I felt afraid of what he would do if I didn't go to him. So I tiptoed a little closer and, just as I got close enough to smell the stale cigarette smoke on his breath, he lunged towards my legs and hooked one arm behind my knees, pulling me towards him.

I stumbled forward as I lost my balance and let out a little cry. Mum didn't stop what she was doing. *What was she doing?*

The man grinned as his eyes swept up and down me, watching as I finally got close enough to see Mum's actions. The man's *thing* was outside of his tracksuit and she had it in her mouth. Her eyes were closed and she didn't seem to be aware that I was right there next to her.

I wanted to scream at her: 'Stop it!'

But I couldn't speak. I was too scared. None of this made any sense to me. I was seven years old and just minutes before I'd been asleep in my bed.

The man appeared to be enjoying my discomfort. He was looking at me hard and I squirmed, self-conscious and embarrassed. Eventually he spoke again: 'I'll have you one day, Annabelle.' His voice was low like a whisper. 'One day, when your periods start, I will have you.'

The moment seemed to last forever. Me standing there, watching my mum, the man grinning at me, his bony, cold fingers wrapped around the back of my bare legs. Finally he let his arm drop and nodded his head towards the stairs: 'You can go to bed now.'

And with that I bolted. My heart was beating hard as I flew up the stairs and dived into bed, pulling the duvet over my head, closing my eyes tight. I wanted to go to sleep straight away, forget all about the man and what I'd just seen. But it took some time before I was calm enough to relax. I kept going over and over it in my head. I didn't understand what I'd seen or anything the man had said. It just didn't make sense.

That was my first encounter with Colin Batley. And though I would come to learn later what he meant by his words, I never forgot that first terrifying night.

Chapter 2

Mum

I don't ever remember a time when my mother was kind to me. My younger sister and I were never kissed or cuddled. She didn't tuck us in at night telling us how much she loved us. She didn't read to us or play with us. She barely even spoke to us. In fact, my mum's presence in my life was so light that until the age of seven I barely remember her being there at all.

Tall and slim with long, auburn hair, Mum had a tattoo of a shark on her shoulder and, looking back now, that is what she was like during those early years. She glided silently through my childhood like a shark: a sleek, dark and brooding presence; a vaguely threatening outline on my horizon. Occasionally when I turn my inner gaze towards the movement in my memory, I try to look at her, but no, she's gone. Nothing but the ripple of the waters to indicate she was there at all.

Mum was the middle child of three sisters from East London and, before we moved to Wales, I was always round at my mum's older sister, Aunt Becca's house. Aunt Becca was different from my mum. She was round and warm where my mum was thin and cold. Best of all, she was lovely to me – she would take me to the park and we'd have picnics together. We'd watch films curled up on the sofa in each other's arms and she even took me on holiday with her and her partner, Alex.

One time, we went to stay at a caravan park in Devon and the whole field flooded. It was a strange holiday, marching round in wellies the whole time, but I remember laughing a lot. Aunt Becca had a sparkly sort of laugh, which came often and easily.

Aunt Becca didn't have any children of her own but I knew she wanted them one day, and whenever we were together she practised being a good mummy by showering me with love. I drank it in like water.

'You're *my* daughter really,' she'd say, winking at me, as she hugged me tight. That was our little joke together – we would pretend that Aunt Becca was actually my real mummy and Mum was just the woman I lived with. In some ways, that felt more real to me than the truth. There were never picnics, films or fun things to do at my house. I don't even remember having any toys. My parents had split up when I was two and, a couple of years later, Mum met a new boyfriend, Alan. He was a lot younger than her – just nineteen when she was twenty-four – but he was kind and sweet and together they had my sister, Olivia, who was five years younger than me. It was Alan who picked me up from school every day and often took me to the park.

Tall, stocky and with a shaved head, Alan was happy and lively most of the time. I liked him. It was Alan who took me to my aunt's house at the weekend, who tied the shoelaces on my bright-red trainers and who picked me up from school every day. And it was Alan who tucked me into bed and gave me a kiss goodnight. But I didn't call him 'Daddy' – I knew my real daddy. His name was David, and once or twice a month he'd pick me up to spend the day at his house with his new wife and baby boy.

They had a big garden with a swingball set and a trampoline – I could spend hours playing in that garden. Every time Dad walked me home he loved to scare me by telling me that the place where they were building the new Docklands Light Railway Station was actually the secret lair of the Bogie Man. I'd scream my head off. It wasn't real fear, of course – just the funny, enjoyable fear of a good scare story. It was shouting out 'Boo' when someone came round a corner, riding a roller coaster or being chased up the stairs. It was funny scary. The kind that made you scream then laugh. I didn't know what proper fear was back then.

When Daddy left me at the foot of my block of flats, his smile would flicker with sadness.

'I'll see you again really soon,' he'd say, poking at the freckles on my face. 'Spider poo', that's what he'd call them, and then he'd laugh like mad when I screwed up my face and made a puking sound.

That was my daddy. He was kind and silly and I did love him, but it was Alan who was there for me every day.

So the truth was I wasn't short on love back then. I had my aunts, my dad, Alan and, for everything else, there was always Nan and Granddad. Nan was a tiny little lady – even at a young age I could see that she was small and terribly thin. But she had the same unusual hair colour as me – reddish brown – and she was definitely the boss of the house.

Granddad, with his old-fashioned moustache, looked like Blakey from *On the Buses* – all big and loud and full of jokes. He and Nan would take me with them to their bowls tournaments at the weekends and I loved watching them play in their crisp white shirts and trousers. They were really good, the two of them, and their house was packed full of medals and trophies they'd won through the years.

Christmases were always spent at their house, when Granddad would push all the tables together to make room for the whole family to eat their dinner. He called it his 'Star Trek' table. Granddad loved his drink and he enjoyed clowning around, pretending to walk into doors or stutter to make me laugh and spit out my Ribena.

I loved being with my granddad – in the holidays he'd take me to the beach at Southend and we'd sit and lick the melting ice cream from our sticky hands. Or we'd go up to London to visit the museums and, afterwards, he'd put me on his shoulders while he pointed out all the exciting sights of the city. Granddad worked on the reception desk of a university and sometimes he took me to see the building, which was huge and very busy. On the tube on the way home we'd play I Spy until I'd drop off, exhausted, sprawled out over his legs.

Later, we would sneak into the kitchen together and raid the fridge – eating sweet pink ham straight out of the packet, even though we knew Nan hated us doing that. Nan and Granddad always had lovely food in their fridge – ham, cocktail sausages and Mini Babybels. In the cake tin there were cherry bakewell tart slices, my favourite.

I don't remember having nice food at my house – it was always Smart Price food from Asda. Alan used to call it 'the upside-down house' because the bedrooms were in the ground floor and the living room was upstairs. It wasn't a house at all really; it was a maisonette in a large block of high-rise flats. We were on Floor 14 and had to get a lift up to our place every day.

I look back now through these memories, searching for my mum, but I can't see her anywhere. I don't see her in our 'upside-down house', I don't see her at the Star Trek table at Christmas, and I don't see her at the park near our home. All I can see is the shadow of her. People tell me that in London she was a good mum, that she looked after me and my sister well. I believe she even held down a job as a dental nurse at one point. But I have barely any memories of her at all before our move to Wales, and before Colin Batley arrived in our lives. So I don't know if she changed after she met Colin or if I just can't remember the good stuff that happened before him because of everything that came after. All I can say for certain is that Mum definitely started to make her mark in my life after Colin arrived on the scene. And not for good reasons.

A few days after that midnight encounter, I woke up desperate for a wee. The house we were living in at the time wasn't just poorly decorated; it was also laid out in a very odd way. There was one toilet, which could only be accessed through the living room. But for some reason we had a lock on our living room door. I ran down the stairs to try the living room door – it was locked. So I ran back upstairs and opened my mum's door. She was in bed, duvet pulled up to her chin, her long hair pooled around her head.

'Mum, I need to go to the toilet,' I whispered urgently.

'Hmmmm?' Mum moaned, but she didn't open her eyes. I crouched next to her head and winced as I felt the sharp pressure on my bladder.

'Please, Mum, please open the living room door. I need a wee. It's an emergency.'

Mum turned her head over: 'Go away.'

'But I need to go now! I really, really need it.'

I was desperate and crossed my legs, trying hard to hold it in.

'In a minute,' she mumbled at me.

'Mum, please!' I begged. I was bobbing up and down on the spot, both arms dug in between my legs, trying desperately to hold the wee which I knew had to come out soon.

'Just go away. I'll be there in a minute,' she growled from the other side of her bed. I knew she'd not even opened her eyes the whole time I was there. I tried to clench hard but it was useless.

'Please, Mum. I really need to go.' I was crying now. There was nothing I could do. I could feel the warm liquid start to dribble down my leg and, once it started, I couldn't stop it. I stood there in silence and horror as a large puddle of urine collected at my feet.

A minute passed. Mum must have sensed I was still there. She sat up and groggily put a hand through her hair, pushing it out of her eyes. She looked at me, wet and humiliated at the side of her bed.

'What the fuck have you done, you stupid girl?' she yelled. 'I said "wait a minute". Why didn't you just wait before pissing all over my bloody floor?'

I couldn't look at her.

'I tried but it was an emergency,' I replied quietly, full of shame. Now the tears really started to come. I couldn't help these either. They poured out of me.

'It's no good bloody crying now, you stupid little bitch!' she shouted, jumping out of bed. She came round to examine the rapidly cooling yellow liquid seeping into the floorboards.

'Look what you've done!' She walloped me then round the back of my head. 'Just look what you've done!' And with that she struck me again, so forcefully this time I stumbled forward, stepping in my wee, making it splash up my pyjama bottoms. She kept hitting me about the head and back as I cowered under her, trying to put my arms and legs up to protect myself, the tears still streaming down my face. I ran into my room, my pyjama trousers wet and sticking to my legs, still whimpering: 'I couldn't hold it in. I couldn't hold it in.'

I didn't like Wales from the start. It was a big change from our previous life in London. At first we lived with another family but after a while we moved into the house where I met Colin for the first time and later did the wee on the floor. The house was disgusting and a few months later we moved again. I had started at a new primary school by this time but it was hard to fit in and

I missed my old life, the familiar places and all the family we left behind.

At first my dad called up every Saturday to speak to me but, as time moved on, he stopped phoning so often. At least, that's what my mum told me. Sometimes I'd hear the phone ring and Mum would pick it up quickly. I'd hear angry whispers and then, seconds later, the sound of the receiver slamming down in its cradle.

'Was that my dad?' I'd call out.

'Nope,' she'd reply.

Nobody came to visit us, so I missed seeing my nan, granddad and aunties. At first Alan was there, making the adjustment easier, but after a while he left too. When I asked my mum where he was, she told me he'd gone away to work in Oxford. He'd pop up every now and then but the time between each visit seemed to get longer and longer. I couldn't understand it. I know I wasn't his child but Olivia was his daughter. Why wasn't he around any more? In his place, Mum took over the job of looking after us. Only she really couldn't be bothered to do much, so there were no more trips to the park or games of hide and seek. There were certainly no kisses goodnight.

Mum didn't work – she was on benefits but, even so, she didn't seem to have any time for anything or anybody except the new person I met on that strange night in July. I learned his name was Colin, and he would often come round and the two of them would disappear into her room for hours at a time. She was completely wrapped up in him and what little she did for us was done grudgingly. The oven chips she cooked were often burnt and the beans cold. She didn't take us anywhere or meet anyone new and, most of the time, when Colin wasn't there, she just lounged on the sofa watching TV or slept in bed. As a consequence I was miserable and lonely.

One Saturday morning, still just a few months after the move, I decided I'd had enough. I was going to go and find my daddy. So I packed a few clothes into an Asda carrier bag, put on my grey coat and went downstairs. Mum glanced up from the TV – she was smoking and watching *Live and Kicking* while my sister toddled around. Her eyes flickered to the carrier bag at my side.

'Where are you going?' she asked.

'I'm going to live with my dad.'

I didn't say what I was thinking: that I didn't like her any more. That she wasn't very nice to me and she didn't seem to be bothered to do anything.

'OK,' she replied. 'I'll arrange it.'

I set my carrier bag full of clothes down in the hallway and sat on the sofa in the living room in my coat, ready to go. I really believed Mum when she said she was going to arrange for me to go and live with my dad. I was surprised. She seemed so matter-of-fact about it. I'd expected a fight, so I was relieved and happy at her calm response. She got up and went into the kitchen, where I heard her speaking quietly on the phone and, about an hour later, that strange man Colin came to the house and plonked himself next to me on the sofa.

Just like the first time I saw him, I noticed the gaps in his mouth where his teeth should have been when he started talking: 'So, I've been speaking to your mum. Tell me, why do you want to go and live with your dad?'

He leant his long body back against the sofa, so I had to twist myself round to face him.

'I just do,' I replied. 'I want to see my dad. I like it in London. I don't like it here.'

'Well, you know, if you want to go to London, that's fine,' Colin replied, sliding a cigarette from a pack he took from his jacket pocket. 'That's your choice and I'll take you there myself right now if you like. We'll go in my car. Today.'

He looked at me then, expectantly, like I just had to say the word and he would jump up and drive me to London. But I knew there was more coming. He stuck the cigarette between his lips, lit it from a black plastic lighter he pulled out of his tracksuit bottoms and inhaled deeply.

'But, you know, it will be horrible living with him.' He exhaled a dense plume of smoke into my face. 'The thing is, your dad won't really look after you properly. Not like your mum. He won't be bothered to take care of you, feed you and wash your clothes and take you to school. But, as I said, it's your choice and if you want to I'll take you there now.'

I didn't know what to say – I *did* want to go and see my dad. I thought my dad loved me. But I hadn't heard from him in a while now and there was something in the way that Colin spoke that made me doubt my feelings. After all, I couldn't remember the last time he'd called to speak to me on a Saturday night. Maybe Colin was right; maybe my dad didn't really care about me. He had another family now. And if I left, how would I cope without my mum?

Colin fixed me with an intense, hard stare, one eyebrow raised in anticipation of my response. He was wearing the same track-suit bottoms I'd seen him in the first time, the same leather jacket, only today it was a different football top.

'Well? Do you want me to take you right now to your dad's place?'

There was something in the way he was saying it – it was less of a question, more of a threat. I felt like a trapped animal.

I looked up at my mum, who was standing in the corner, watching us both, her arms folded, not saying a word. Why doesn't she speak? I wondered.

Say something, I screamed at her in my head. *SAY SOME-THING!*

But no, she just stood there, eyeing me silently. I squirmed about, not sure how to reply. I really did want to see my dad. I wanted to talk to him at least, but I didn't know how to tell this stranger what I wanted. I wasn't even sure how he fitted into my life. Where was Alan? Where were Nan and Granddad? I wanted to cry.

I felt scared. Scared of this man and scared of leaving my mum. What if Colin was right and Daddy didn't really care about me? Who would look after me then?

'Do you want to go?' he asked again.

I shook my head.

'So, you are going to stay here?' he said.

'Yes,' I replied. 'I, uh, I think I'll stay here.'

'Good girl. I think you made the right choice.'

He slapped the sofa cushion then, as if to indicate that a decision had been made, and our conversation was now over. Then he pushed himself up off the sofa and walked through to the kitchen, my mum trailing behind him.

After he'd gone I felt confused and upset. I'd had the choice to leave but he'd convinced me to stay. I really did want to go but I was too scared. I took my bag of clothes back upstairs and, as I got to the door of my bedroom, I started to cry. I was still miserable, even more than before, because now I didn't think my daddy loved me any more. And I was definitely stuck here with no hope of escape.

Chapter 3

The Church

We moved around a lot at first, but eventually, after a year, we were given our own council house in a small cul-de-sac called Clos Yr Onnen. I could never pronounce our road name – apparently it was Welsh for Ash Tree Close. The funny thing was, it was right next door to Colin's house. It wasn't until we moved in that I even realized he had a family of his own. There was his wife, Elaine, who was really kind and motherly and cooked lovely food, a couple of sons who were both a lot older than me, and a daughter, Hope, whom I recognized from the year above me at primary school, though we had never spoken.

The first time I met Hope I was standing in my front garden and she popped out of a hole in the hedge. The hole was the entrance to a short cut to the main road – a little alleyway with twenty houses on either side which someone had nicknamed 'The Forties'.

'Hello!' she called out, a great big grin on her face. Hope was small like me and very pretty with long, honey-blonde hair. I liked her instantly, with her hair pulled back in a swinging pony-tail, wide smile and shining eyes.

'Hi,' I said, a little shy.

'So you've moved in next door to us?' She nodded towards our semi. I nodded back.

'Well, do you want to come up and play in my room?' she asked and, with that, she dived into her house. I went to follow her – inside it was laid out exactly the same as ours. The front door opened to a hallway with a downstairs toilet as you walked in, and the living room was on the left. The kitchen was straight in front and up the stairs there were two bedrooms, a bathroom and a box room.

Hope had the box room all to herself with a cool cabin bed and toys stuffed into every corner. It was the largest collection of toys I'd ever seen. They were falling off shelves, spilling out of drawers and crammed down the side of her wardrobe. She had dozens of My Little Ponies, cuddly toys and every Barbie imaginable, including all the accessories, the full Barbie wardrobe, house, car, carriages, the lot! And she had tons of her own clothes too. It was like walking into Santa's Grotto and we played for ages with all her brilliant toys.

'Where did you get all of this?' I breathed, in awe, as I tried to pull Barbie's arm through a pink sequined ball gown.

'My dad gets them for me,' she said casually. 'Dad will get anything I ask.'

And you know what – she was right. Hope was the baby of the house – with boys coming before her, she was the apple of her daddy's eye. There was nothing he wouldn't do for her.

From the moment I met Hope my life changed for the better. It didn't take long for me to forget all about running away or that strange, candlelit encounter with Colin. We had a new life now – we were part of something more than just our small little family. Hope's dad was the leader of our Church, which was called the Church of the BPH, although nobody ever told me what BPH stood for. Apart from Hope's family and us there were two women who lived in our cul-de-sac who also belonged to the Church, and two other families who lived nearby, so from the moment I moved into Ash Tree Close, I stopped being lonely.

Sandra lived across the road and you could see her house from ours. She was nice and friendly. Shelley, meanwhile, lived right down the other end of the cul-de-sac and she was loud and bossy and reminded me of a man. They had known Colin in London and I gradually found out that they had met in London and moved to Wales at the same time.

Then there were the other members of the Church who didn't live in the cul-de-sac, but were nevertheless around all the time. There was Orla, a short lady who wore glasses who was about my mum's age and had two daughters – Millie and Fiona. Millie was the same age as me – she was really sporty and tall and Fiona, who was a year older, was quite shy. They had a brother, Thomas, who I saw only occasionally – he was about five years older than me. Then there was Griff, a big bloke with a straggly beard who worshipped Colin. Griff's son Pete was disabled, but you couldn't really tell just by looking at him. He had learning difficulties but he was really sweet and I liked to play with him because whatever game you were playing, he always let you win. And he had the funniest laugh.

From the word go the Church families were together all the time, so there were always loads of kids around to play with. It made life a lot easier for me than just being stuck inside with my mum. Sometimes it felt like I was in Hope's house more than my own. It was certainly easier to ask her mum Elaine for something than it was to ask mine. I didn't bother any more – if I was hungry I'd go to Hope's house and get fed there.

At first, Hope and I went in and out through each other's front doors, but after a while Colin knocked down the garden fence between our houses so we had access via the back. Very quickly we became inseparable. Hope was more than a friend to me; she was like a sister, and the Church my new family. Colin was no longer the strange, scary man from that first time we met – he was my best friend's dad, someone who enjoyed having a good time.

Special times of the year were now celebrated together – Colin's family hosted Christmas and Easter and put on big roast dinners followed by cakes baked by Elaine and, in the summer, Colin put up a bouncy castle in our joint garden and we had barbecues in the evening. But his favourite time of the year was Halloween. Halloween was really special to Colin.

Each year we'd get dressed up and go round to Colin's place for a big party. The first year I went as a witch and I couldn't believe it when I walked in to see the whole house had been done up with fake spider webs, bats dangling from doorframes, fake blood on the walls and a massive skeleton hanging from a ball in the hallway. I'd never seen anything like it. Elaine had made loads of delicious cakes, there was music and dancing, and all the kids were allowed to stay up late. Of course it was just the Church families and there was no drinking – that was one of the Church rules – but it didn't make any difference to us. Later on, all us kids put on a talent show for the adults. Hope and I did a dance routine together and we won!

I was very young then, so all the Church stuff didn't really interest me. All I knew was what I saw in our houses, like the pictures and statues of Egyptian gods. Colin had put up pictures in our living room very early on – one featured a gold mask of a man with a funny beard, slanted eyes and a blue striped head-dress. This was Tutankhamen, said Colin. Two other pictures showed people in white robes with dog faces or bird heads and picture writing that Colin said was called hieroglyphics. All the Church families had the same pictures on their living room walls and one of the rules was that we weren't allowed to turn our back on them. So if we were sitting in that room we couldn't be sitting with our back to the pictures and, when we left the room, we all had to walk slightly backwards.

One day Colin tried to explain the pictures to me, but I was only half-listening. Slumped in his armchair, with a fag stuck in his face, he pointed one by one to the figures in the pictures:

'The one with the head of the cat – she's called Bastet, the Goddess of War and the protector of the underworld. Horus, there, the one with the head of the falcon, the bird – he is the Protector God. If you have an Eye of Horus, you will always be protected by the Gods. Ra, the one with the sun on his head, he is the Creator – the solar deity. He rules all parts of the world

– the Realm, the Palace and the Abyss. And Anubis there, the one with the dog head, he is the God of the Afterlife.'

I nodded, trying to show I was listening, but none of it really went in. I knew I had to pretend because Colin was so important in our Church and everyone else cared a lot about the things Colin said. Since Colin was the High Priest, he was almost like a god himself. If Colin said 'tea' and looked at someone, then that person had to make him tea. That's just the way it was.

He had two Rottweilers in his house and they always went everywhere with him. I didn't like them much – they were always jumping up and barking in your face. One was called Toots, after Tutankhamen, and the other was named Sekhet, after the Egyptian lion god. But Colin always said they were the devil's dogs.

'They are the Dogs of Hell!' Colin would laugh, as I backed away from them one day. 'Satan's own canines, the devil's dogs! So, do you think I'm the devil, Annabelle?'

I gave him a small, scared smile but I couldn't tell if he was joking or not.

Though most of the time they were fine, Colin had trained his Rottweilers to attack. If he stood next to you and started saying, 'Ow, ow, ow', they would growl and get ready to attack. But then he could call them off if he liked. He always laughed, saying he was only messing around, but you could never be certain. Those dogs had big teeth.

My mum thought Colin was the bees' knees and she always did everything he said. Sometimes at night she'd go round to his place for long meetings that went on for hours. I used to dread those nights – she'd leave us in the house on our own and, even though I knew she was only next door, it was still scary to be left by ourselves.

Mum had a little shelf in her bedroom that she called her altar – on it were a number of dark metal statues of the Egyptian gods, each about 30 centimetres tall. Every day she spent an hour in her room, kneeling in front of her altar, meditating.

'I'm doing my meds now!' she'd shout out to me, as she walked up the stairs. 'Just watch your sister and make sure you don't come in.'

I knew she did this meditation stuff naked because once I accidentally walked in on her. She was kneeling down with her head on the floor, making strange repetitive noises. It was then I saw her tattoo – she had a bizarre symbol imprinted on her arm that looked like a cross with a bubble on the top.

'It's the ankh,' she explained later. 'The ancient symbol of life.'

Gradually I found out that all the women in the Church had one of these, and also tattoos of the Eye of Horus, which meant they were protected, and they also wore upside-down crosses round their necks.

Not everyone's tattoos looked the same, though – I noticed that some had different colours around them. Mum said the colour symbolized each person's rank in the Church. Hers was dark mauve, which apparently meant she was very high-ranking. She said this proudly. I know it meant a lot to her.

In fact, the Church meant a lot to me too. My life was governed by its rules, and one of the biggest was not being allowed to mix with outsiders. So, apart from playing with Church kids in each other's houses, we weren't allowed to play outside or visit non-Church members' homes. We weren't even allowed to go to the park or walk to the shop. I suppose it didn't matter that much because I didn't have any money to buy stuff anyway. We were poor, I knew that. Mum was on benefits – in fact, all the women in our Church were on benefits – so buying stuff wasn't something I thought about. Most days I'd come in from school, dump my stuff in the hallway, change out of my school clothes and then go straight round to Hope's to play with her. Being with Hope was great – it made me forget about Mum and how stern she was. By now I could barely talk to her. She never asked me how my day was or talked to me about anything. There was no communication, no conversation. She lived for Colin and the Church.

Though it was great to have new people in my life I couldn't forget about the family we'd left behind. I missed my nan and granddad so much. It was well over a year before they came to visit. They caught the train from London to our house in Wales – Granddad said it took them five hours and they had to leave really early in the morning, when it was still dark. We showed them round the house when they arrived and I was very proud to show them the room I shared with Olivia. My single bed ran along the wall with the window, next to a tallboy cupboard, while Olivia's cot was pushed into the recess made by the boiler.

We stayed in the house that day because Mum didn't want us going outdoors to play but I didn't mind. It was just nice to see

Nan and Granddad and they'd brought me some pens and a colouring book.

'Why didn't you use the disposable camera I sent you?' Nan asked Mum over lunch. It was just ham sandwiches and some crisps — Mum hadn't gone to too much trouble. Quickly I looked up from my plate. I remembered the little yellow and black camera Nan had sent in the post. I'd had great fun running round our new home, snapping away at Olivia and Mum in different parts of the house. I even took a couple of pictures of Hope.

'Oh that?' Mum took a sip of her squash. 'I don't know what happened to that camera. I think it got lost.'

I kept my mouth shut. I knew for a fact the camera wasn't lost. After I'd taken a couple of pictures of Hope, posing with her biggest, cheesiest grin, Colin asked me what I was doing.

'Nan gave us a camera to take some pictures to send to her,' I explained. 'It's so they can see our new home and how much me and my baby sister have grown up.'

'I see,' Colin scowled, then he held out his hand expectantly. I gave him the camera and never saw it again. When I asked my mum later what had happened to it, she said: 'That camera isn't allowed in the Church. It's against our rules.'

'But it wasn't our camera. It was Nana's camera.'

'Shut it,' Mum snapped back. And that was the end of the conversation.

I was so sad when it came time for Nan and Granddad to leave.

'Why can't they stay here tonight?' I begged my mum in the

hallway, as she went to get their coats. They had come such a long way to see us. I didn't understand why they couldn't stay a little longer. Poor Nan looked so tired.

'It's not allowed,' Mum hissed at me.

'But why?' I wheedled.

'That's what Colin says. It's Church rules, so just shut up.'

And that was that – end of discussion. So they took the train all the way back to London that same night, getting in at 2 a.m. No wonder they never came back and, of course, Mum didn't take us on any visits, so I didn't see my grandparents again until I left Wales a decade later.

The only other person from our former life was Alan. He was part of our Church at first, and he still came round from time to time, but gradually the visits petered out. Mum didn't seem to like having him around any more, so when he was back in the area he would stay at one of the other houses. This didn't go on long – gradually he stopped coming to see us too and he moved out of the area altogether.

I suppose I didn't notice so much any more – I had good friends at school and Hope was my friend at home so everything, as far as I knew, was normal. Yes, we were part of a church but other people had religion in their lives too, so it didn't seem unusual. The only difference was that our church had its own set of rules – like we weren't allowed to swear, mix with other children, go into boys' rooms or look at Colin directly in his eyes.

'You have to be careful,' he warned me, when he told me that rule. 'You don't want to see what's in my eyes. If you stare too much you'll see into the Abyss, a place where there is nothing but suffering. A lifetime of suffering.'

At the time I found that frightening, so I was really careful not to look Colin in the eyes for the next few days. But there were times I forgot, of course, and, occasionally, if I stared into his eyes, Colin would snap at me: 'Getting a good look into the Abyss? Can you see the devil in there? He can see you!'

I was naughty only once, and that was when I went to a friend's house instead of going to school. My friend Lilly lived right next door to school and one day I bunked off to play at her house. Of course, Mum found out pretty quickly because the school called to tell her I hadn't been in that day and she told Colin. He gave me the slipper that time.

Colin had a red slipper with a hard leather sole and, if we were naughty, we got hit with it. I only got it the once but it really hurt.

He brought the leather sole down hard on each palm, twice, and on the soles of my feet, and they stung for the rest of the day. I was also grounded for six weeks. I don't think it was the bunking off he minded so much as going to my friend's house. Mixing with outsiders was forbidden and I didn't do anything like that again. I certainly didn't like the slipper. I saw Colin give it to his sons all the time. The one person who usually managed to avoid Colin's temper was Hope – and she could get away with murder.

While Colin's boys were always shouted at and told off, Hope was treated like a princess. As for me, I tried to stay out of his way, especially if he was in a bad mood. Colin's bad moods were terrible. They'd hang in the air like a bad smell, making everyone nervous and uncomfortable. Then, out of the blue, he'd leap from his chair towards his victim, his hand raised high, as if he was going to strike. At the last minute he'd stop, his hand suspended inches from their face. The person on the receiving end of this sudden threat was always so shocked that they flinched and cowered with the expectation of the pain – and this made Colin laugh. Colin was big, too – 6 feet 3 inches – so if he hit you, you really knew it. The funny thing was, I never once saw Colin actually strike someone but you could never tell. That's the thing – his temper was so sudden and unpredictable that it could be very unnerving.

I knew that if I was with Hope I'd be OK because he loved her so much and he was always kind to her. I suppose Colin was a bit like my dad – he was the one who made all the decisions about my life; he told me off if I broke the rules, and it was him who gave my mum money each week to get our food. Mum would go and get her benefits once a week and Colin said she was allowed to put £20 each on the gas and electric and the rest had to go to him. Once a fortnight he'd give her £50 and she could go to Asda for her big shop.

As I saw it back then, the only difference between our religion and other people's religions was that we weren't allowed to talk about ours. Colin said that our rules were 'governed under Church secrecy'. I wasn't quite sure what this meant, except we weren't allowed to tell anyone about the rules or even that we had rules! So, if I was invited over to play at a friend's house from school or for a birthday party, not only could I not go, but

I couldn't tell them it was because the Church didn't allow it. I had to say I was busy or that my mum couldn't pick me up.

Similarly, I wasn't allowed to invite anyone back to my house or have a birthday party. Not that my mum would even think about throwing me a party. She didn't do stuff like that – no, I only ever got a birthday card from her, one which always said the same thing: 'Happy Birthday, from Mum and Olivia'. No kisses, not even 'love from'. Nothing. She never got me a cake or presents. I didn't mind – I'd never had anything like that from her so I suppose it didn't bother me.

At Christmas time we all went round to Colin's house and he got us our presents – we were allowed three gifts each: one big thing and two small things. I'm pretty sure Hope got more than that because her room was overflowing with toys, but I didn't mind. I played so much in her room anyway that I never wanted stuff for myself. She was generous – if she didn't want a toy she'd let me have it and, if she had clothes she'd grown out of, she passed them on to me.

One Christmas I got a small TV and video player for my bedroom, which I loved. It sat on my tallboy. It didn't have an ariel plugged in, so I borrowed some Disney films from Hope and at night I'd go to my room, lie on my bed and watch *The Little Mermaid*, *The Lion King* and *Aladdin*. We both loved Disney and watched these films obsessively over and over again until we could repeat whole chunks of dialogue and sing the songs word for word.

At the end of our second summer in Wales, all the Church families went on holiday to France. It was so exciting – my first real holiday abroad! At the beginning of September we piled into three cars, took the ferry across the Channel, and stayed in a caravan park near Euro Disney. The girls had one caravan, the boys another and the adults stayed in a third. Every day we were allowed to go on loads of different rides, which was so much fun. We had to go around in a massive crocodile, all of us holding hands. Of course, Hope and I stuck together like glue. We screamed and laughed so much, it was the best time I'd ever had. I loved it. Colin bought me a special cap too with Goofy on it.

From then on we went to France at the end of every summer, usually at the same time as the schools went back, so all us kids missed the first week of the new term. For some reason this bunking off was OK because Colin said so – and for reasons I'll never know, none of the schools ever questioned why so many children from the same cul-de-sac were all off at the same time. I didn't think about it much back then – the important thing was, I was going on holiday. And if we'd never met Colin or become part of his Church, good things like that just wouldn't be happening to me. Yes, I truly loved our new life and my 'new sister' Hope.

So when I left primary school, aged eleven, I was looking forward to a long, fun summer with the bouncy castle in the garden followed by a trip to Euro Disney before starting my new secondary school. I was happy, excited at the prospect of nearly two months of doing nothing, just hanging round with Hope and having fun. I had no idea what Colin had planned for me; no clue that my role in the Church was about to get a lot more involved.

Chapter 4

The First Test

'Where are you going?' Hope yelled, as I bumped off the bouncy castle and headed indoors. My limbs felt sticky against the canvas and my head was starting to swim in the blazing sunshine.

'Inside. I'm too hot!' I called back, pushing out my bottom lip and blowing hard to try and direct some cold air up towards my forehead. The tiles on our kitchen floor felt nice and chilly against my bare feet. Beads of sweat pricked at my temples then trickled down past my eyes. I wiped them away with the back of my arm. It was good to be out of the sun's insistent rays.

It was a beautiful day in July but I'd never been very good in the heat. Hope and I had been on the bouncy castle all morning and now I was burning up. I knew I needed a little time indoors to chill out so I could go out and play later. I padded up the stairs to my room, then threw myself on my duvet and closed my eyes. If I lay really still I knew I'd be able to cool down a little.

It couldn't have been more than a minute before I heard a

voice in the room. Startled, my eyes flickered open and I sat bolt upright.

'What was that?' I asked groggily.

'I said – what are you doing inside on a day like this?' Colin asked, as he sat down next to me on the bed.

'I'm too hot,' I told him.

'Don't you like the bouncy castle?'

'Yes, I do.'

'Well, what's the matter then? Why are you indoors?'

'I just don't like to get too hot, that's all. It makes me feel ill.'

'Mmm hmm,' he said, nodding his head. 'I see.'

Colin was wearing his navy tracksuit bottoms and football top, as usual, and he leaned in close to me, so close I could smell the strangely sweet scent of stale tobacco, tangy, like old sweat, that engulfed him like a cloud. He smoked Dorchesters almost constantly; it was rare to see him without one on the go. He was looking at me and there was no change in his voice or composure, as he suddenly reached out, put his hands on my shoulders and pushed me back on the bed.

'Yes, it's very hot today, isn't it?' he said, as he pinned me down, his long body now pushing itself between my legs. I was frightened. I didn't know what was going on, as he held an arm across my chest to stop me wriggling.

I felt helpless. I could barely move for the weight of him.

I didn't know where to look or what to do. *Why was he doing this?*

I looked over at the door – it was wide open. From out of the window below us I heard the shouts of the children as they bounced up and down in the sun. Over the top of that, the constant whir of the generator. The window was only slightly ajar, just as far as the child lock would allow.

Colin's clammy hand pushed my knickers and shorts to one side. I looked down. He had his *thing* over the waistband of his tracksuit bottoms. Now he wriggled to push my legs out and he thrust himself inside me in one forceful movement.

Oh my God. The pain!

I wanted to scream. It burned inside me like a red-hot poker.

But Colin's expression never changed. He simply adjusted himself so he had one arm underneath my neck and the other arm against the bed, as he slid himself inside me again and again. I was terrified.

What the hell was going on?

My eyes watered from the pain. Colin didn't say anything – he just looked at me, like he was waiting for something. And still that awful stench surrounded me – it filled my nostrils and made me want to retch. I couldn't stand it any more.

I turned my head away. I looked at the wallpaper, the strange blue wallpaper with the clouds on, and I tried to imagine myself floating away on those clouds. The children's voices echoed in my head now, as I tried to block out what was happening to me.

What's going on? What is this? It hurts. God, it hurts!

My curtains fluttered with a light breeze, the awful white curtains with red flowers on them that my mum had made from bed sheets. *What's happening? Why won't it stop?*

He pushed again and again and then, after what felt like ages, he just stopped.

It can't have lasted more than a minute but the pain went on and on. Colin's face had remained set throughout. He eased himself off me and sat back on the bed.

'I told you I'd have you,' was all he said in his usual toneless voice. No expression in his voice or on his face.

I swallowed hard – I wanted to cry. It felt like someone had kicked me in the privates. I couldn't move. I was too terrified to do anything.

'Right, now sort yourself out and go downstairs,' he said dismissively, as he got up and walked out. Then he was gone, out of the bedroom door that had been open the whole time.

At that moment I felt nothing but relief. It was over – whatever he had done to me was over and he was gone. I lay there for a little while, too scared to move. Why had Colin hurt me like that? I just didn't understand. Bizarrely, I knew from that moment I couldn't tell anybody what had happened. Colin was the leader in our Church; he was like a God himself, he had told us so. If he did things, it was always for a reason. In any case, I couldn't tell my mum anything; she just didn't care. And this was Elaine's husband. I couldn't tell her. It was Hope's daddy – I wasn't going to tell her. So I just lay there feeling very alone.

After a bit, I pulled my shorts back into place and sat up, wincing as I felt a sharp stinging sensation down there. I desperately needed to go to the toilet but I was frightened of what I might discover if I did. I was frightened of seeing myself all red and swollen. So I just hobbled out of the house and went outside to play with the others.

'Aren't you coming on the bouncy castle?' Hope shouted to me, as she bounced up and down. I'd been sat on the grass for the last ten minutes, still in too much pain to move.

'In a minute,' I called, putting on a fake smile for her. 'I'm still hot.'

I lied instantly and easily. Of course I did. I didn't know what had happened or why, but I knew it was almost certainly governed under Church secrecy.

For the rest of the day I moved very carefully, but I was even more careful to stay next to Hope. Now I knew what her daddy could do, I didn't want to give him another opportunity to get me alone. Down there, it throbbed and throbbed. It felt like I'd been ripped apart – and in some ways I had been. When finally the need became too great and I went to the toilet, I saw blood in my knickers. I wanted to cry then. I was only eleven years old.

That night we all ate together outside – Colin was on the barbecue while Elaine and Shelley buttered white baps and ladled out beans from a large mixing bowl. The setting sun cast long shadows from the bouncy castle over us all. Still wearing my flimsy yellow shorts and vest top, I shivered in the cool air.

'What do you want, Anna?' Colin called out to me, the ever-present fag dangling unappetizingly over the sizzling meat. 'Burger or sausage?' He was flipping burgers and turning sausages expertly, like this was normal. Like everything was normal.

WHAT DID YOU DO TO ME? I wanted to scream at him. How could he behave like nothing had happened? It was crazy.

I tried to act normally too but I couldn't look at him all

evening. I didn't eat much either and, later, when we were watching TV, I disappeared into myself, exhausted from fighting the pain all day.

It was a relief to go to bed that night, so at least I could lie down and rest but I didn't get much sleep. Suddenly that first candlelit encounter with Colin came back to me. Is this what he meant when he talked to me that first time? In the years that had passed I'd almost forgotten about that midnight meeting with my mum kneeling in front of his lap. It had been replaced with my experience of Colin as the Church leader, as my best mate's dad, my neighbour and my mum's friend. Now his words and my fear came flooding back.

But why had this happened now? During that candlelit speech he'd said he would 'have me' when I started my period. I hadn't started my period yet. I was only eleven. *Why does he want to hurt me? Is it because I've done something wrong?* The questions chased themselves round and round in my head all night long. That pungent stench of stale Dorchesters on his breath kept coming back to me, making me want to vomit. Finally, in the early hours of the morning, I drifted off, but when I woke with the sunlight, I caught a whiff of that smell again on my pillow and my heart sank.

It still comes back to me today – that foul stench. I can taste it in my mouth for no reason at all. One minute I'm sitting watching TV, everything is fine, and the next minute the smell leaks into my nostrils. And then I'm back there, eleven years old again, pinned to my bed, helpless and frightened.

Why is he doing this? Why?

Chapter 5

A Summer of Tests

I didn't have to wait long for the answer. The next morning Colin walked into our house laden down with rolls and rolls of green and cream striped wallpaper. Mum was lying on the couch in the living room, smoking and watching *Fifteen to One*.

'Colin's going to decorate the house,' Mum explained, wafting her hand in the air, but not lifting her eyes from the TV.

'Got to make this place presentable,' Colin said, nodding at our disgusting brown walls, hitching up his tracksuit bottoms. I don't know what he meant by that – it's not like we ever had guests round. The only ones who came in our home were his family.

The moment I set eyes on Colin again, I felt a strange twisting sensation in my stomach. I felt nervous, uncertain. Colin was a different person now. He wasn't the man I knew as Hope's dad any more, he was the person who hurt me. The day went on as normal but, in the evening, as soon as Mum put Olivia down for the night, she disappeared next door to play PlayStation.

'Colin should be here soon,' she said, grabbing her fags from the kitchen counter and darting out the back door. As the door slammed behind her, I felt a chill of fear and I knew what I had to do. I went upstairs and got changed into my pink and yellow striped pyjamas. I didn't want to be around when Colin arrived. Besides, I was tired from my sleepless night. I turned out the light and curled up under my duvet.

Of course I wasn't really asleep when I heard the back door open twenty minutes later. I listened as a series of clunking noises signalled Colin bringing in a stepladder and depositing various heavy objects on our landing. I listened as his footsteps came and went, the back door of the house slamming shut every time and finally he seemed to pause in the hallway.

Don't come up here, I prayed silently in the dark. *Please don't come up here.*

Creak. Creak. Creak.

The dreadful sound of footsteps on our staircase. The steps got louder and louder. I heard the rattle of the door handle and suddenly a shaft of light broke into the room, making me squint. Colin's long dark silhouette filled the doorframe.

'Come out here, would you?' Colin said in a low voice. I suppose I had been expecting this. I swung my legs out of bed and slowly followed him out to the landing, full of dread.

What now?

Colin had already got himself set up with his stepladder and bucket of glue. He didn't bother stripping off the old stuff. He just started painting over it with glue, a fag jammed into the corner of his mouth.

For a while I just sat on the landing, knees pulled up to my chest, and watched as he prepared the wall to put up a sheet of the paper. As he unfurled the first roll, I noticed a gold rim at the edge of each sheet.

He was so tall that he only needed to go up onto a three-step ladder to reach the top. He lined the paper up against the edge of the ceiling and swept his arms downwards, pushing it into place then running the brush up and down to ensure the glue stuck fast. He worked slowly, very slowly.

'You know, the Gods are pleased with you, Anna,' he said, pressing his palms against the corners of the sheet and leaning into the wall. 'They talk to me. They tell me things. As the Prince Priest I communicate with them directly and they tell me that you are one of the protected ones. You are special.'

I looked down, slightly embarrassed but also quietly pleased. It was nice to think the Gods had noticed me. That they were talking about me. There was silence while Colin kept working. I wanted to know more now but I dared not ask any questions. We weren't allowed to speak to Colin unless he spoke first. He climbed down off the ladder and looked at me like he was trying to make an important decision. He breathed in hard then let out a long sigh.

I wrapped my arms tighter round my knees and looked down.

'You know, Anna, it's vital that you exercise nothing but Pure Will in your life.'

'Yes, I know,' I said. Well, I knew the words at least. I'm not sure I totally understood what Colin meant when he talked about 'Pure Will', but I felt if I listened hard enough eventually I would understand. Colin was much cleverer than anyone else I knew – I was sure he would help me to reach a higher place in our Church. As much as I was frightened of him, I was also flattered that he was giving me so much attention. He was clever and important. I was just a little girl, after all. He returned to brushing down the paper.

'Will is all that matters – all that matters,' he spoke, as if to the wall. 'Everything else is restriction and will bring nothing but eternal pain, a gateway to the Abyss. You hear people talk about sin? About modesty and chastity, about avoiding sin and impurity? Rubbish! It's all rubbish. The idea of sin is restriction, a restriction to the purity of the will. And if you are restricted in your will then you will never reach the Palace.

'Understand this, Anna, there is *nothing* called sin in our Church. No restrictions. There is nothing but love: love is the law. Love under will. Sin is a construct of man to inhibit nature, to obstruct the True Path. And if you wish to reach the Palace and not be sucked into the void of the Abyss, an eternity of pain without end, a lifetime of suffering, then you must obey your will and reject the notion of sin.

'There are four gates to the Palace, as you well know, and to pass through these gates you must have risen within the Church to a higher realm, to become a Priestess. And the only way to do this is to exercise your Pure Will. To find your True Path.'

His words, like waves, simply washed over me – on and on he went. I did try to understand, but every time I thought I caught a wave it simply melted away. Every time I tried to get hold of the meaning, it slipped through my fingers. But I nodded, occasionally answering him – yes, no – but I didn't really understand. I said what I thought he wanted to hear. After all, I didn't want him to think I was stupid. An hour passed – by now I was feeling very tired and I just wanted to go back to bed. *How long does it take to put up one sheet of paper?*

Finally, as he smoothed down the paper, pushing out the last of the air bubbles, he got off the stepladder and strode across the landing, into my mum's bedroom. He didn't have to say anything – I just knew he expected me to follow. He lay down sideways on the bed, propping up his head with one arm. With the other he fished around in his tracksuit bottoms, pulled out the navy-blue packet of Dorchesters, lit one, and then blew the smoke up in the air before bringing his eyes to rest on me. I sat down on the bed next to him, my hands in my lap.

'How do you feel about what happened yesterday?' he asked.

He caught me off-guard – I didn't know what to say or how to react. I felt dreadful – of course I did – but I couldn't tell him that.

'Fine,' I replied quietly.

'Good, good,' Colin said, sucking in another lungful of smoke. I just wanted this to be over, so I said the words I thought he wanted to hear.

'You are very special to us,' he went on, fixing me with his intense stare. Up close I noticed the yellow nicotine stains on the lenses of his brown-rimmed NHS glasses. 'Very special in the Church. I know that the Gods have a lot of good hope for you, Anna. *We* have a lot of hope for you. We believe you are going to do well, that you will rise to become an important member of our Church, someone who can lead others, show them the way, the true way to the Palace.'

His eyes bored into me, staring so hard I felt the colour rise in my cheeks. He reached out a hand, letting his fingers brush through my long hair.

'You have been chosen and you should feel grateful,' he said, as his fingers snaked through my hair. 'The Gods have watched over you because they know you are one of them. They chose this hair, this special red hair for you. They made your eyes look that way, slanted at the corners, just like them. They created you in their image.' Now one of his fingers started winding a strand of my hair round and round till he held it in a tight curl against my head.

'The Goddess Nuit, the goddess of the stars and the sky, she has cast a protective spell over you. She wants you to enter the Palace. Love is the law, love under will. You do want to progress in the Church, don't you, Anna?'

He let go of my hair and I nodded: 'Yes.'

I believed him then. I believed that I was special, that I had been chosen and I did want to progress. I wanted to do well.

'Are you prepared to take the tests to progress along your path towards the Palace?'

I nodded again.

'Because this is the only way you will fulfil your path and your True Will. This is the way to prove yourself to the Gods. To Horus, Bastet, Anubis, Nuit and Isis – to prove you are worthy of the special status they have given you, worthy of entering the Palace. Are you prepared to pass the tests to go higher in the

Church? Just as it is written in *The Book of The Law*. Do you want to take these tests?'

'Yes.'

'Do you have any questions?'

'No.'

He nodded again, seemingly satisfied: 'Good – now get undressed.'

Just then I realized what all of this meant. These things he was doing – they were the tests! I'd just agreed to more of them, before I'd even known what he was talking about. And now I was torn; even though I did really want to progress in the Church, I was still just eleven years old. And I really did *not* want to get undressed in front of a fully grown man, let alone the father of my best friend. Still, I couldn't back out now. So, very slowly, I pulled down my pyjama bottoms first and then slowly slipped my top over my head. Then I sat back on the side of the bed, embarrassed as anything, in my knickers. I always wore knickers in bed.

'Take them off,' Colin ordered. Of course I did as I was told and I felt horrible. I was completely naked now, as Colin told me to lie back on the bed. I cringed as I felt his long cold fingers run up and down my body. I just lay there, looking up at the ceiling, my arms crossed over my chest.

'Put your arms down,' he said.

My arms went down to my side, and I lay there on my mum's bed, rigid, like a plank of wood.

Now Colin stubbed out his cigarette in an overflowing ashtray on the floor, pulled his tracksuit bottoms around his ankles, and wriggled up towards me so his hips were level with my head. Until this moment I'd been fearful of what was about to happen. But then the frightened part of me switched off and I was suddenly numb. My feelings simply turned off, like a light going out in my head. There was nothing I could do to stop this. It was all going to happen anyway. The fear simply disappeared and in its place was, well, nothing. Nothing at all. It was as if I surrendered myself to the situation because there was really nothing else I could do. It was my body but I was no longer there.

Colin pulled my head up now towards his lap, where I saw his penis hard and long in my face.

'Use your mouth,' he ordered and then, in a moment, he put it inside my mouth. I felt his long fingernails tickling my skin. I wanted this to be over as quickly as possible. I wanted him off me. I wanted to be back in my bed, alone. But now my mouth was filled with him and my gagging reflex started to kick in. The taste in my mouth was metallic, like blood. His thing grew inside my mouth, getting bigger and harder. Colin held the back of my head and pushed it towards him again and again, so his thing went down further towards the back of my throat. After a while, he said: 'Use your tongue.'

Use my tongue? For what? How? I couldn't even *feel* my tongue.

But I didn't feel I could say no, or stop. I'd agreed to this. This was the test Colin talked about; this was the way to please the Gods, to get into the Palace. It's not like I could change my mind now.

'Lay down,' he whispered.

Then he got on top of me and I knew what was coming. I felt my body tense up as I realized what he was going to do and this time he had to push himself into me really hard, which hurt even more than last time. Then he started having sex with me, just like he'd done the day before. Only I didn't know it was called sex at the time. I only knew it as a test. I gritted my teeth, kept my eyes fixed on the ceiling, and just waited until it was over, all the while trying to ignore the shooting pains in my private parts and the revolting odour from Colin's mouth.

'Try and relax,' Colin urged. 'Enjoy it.'

His words didn't make sense. Was this really meant to be fun? How was I meant to enjoy it? I really didn't know, so I just let a thin smile flicker over my face and then went back to staring at my mother's ceiling. It hurt so much. I was already so sore from the day before but now the pain seemed to double up inside me. Again and again he pushed himself on top of me. His face was really close to mine now – his expression was set hard. It was the same intense look of concentration as when he was papering our walls. I couldn't look him in the eye, so I turned my head to stare at the altar in the corner, mentally naming all the statues of the Gods as he thrust himself into me. *Horus. Oww. Anubis. Oww. Isis. Oww. When will it end? When will it end?*

'Try to enjoy it,' he grunted again. It was another order, I realized then. I wasn't meant to actually enjoy it. I was meant to simply do as I was told. So I nodded, acknowledging his command. Then I went back to concentrating on the pain.

I don't know how long it went on for this time – it could have been minutes but it felt like forever. And, just like before, when he decided it was over, he just stopped without any warning – there was no change in his demeanour or expression.

'That will do for tonight,' he said, as he pushed himself off me.

I stared at him, still not really connected to my body or what was going on in the room.

'These are the tests you will have to pass to enter the Palace. Do you want to do them?'

Silence.

No, no, no! I screamed silently in my head.

'Yes,' I said. I sat on the edge of the bed again, now naked, embarrassed and sore. Colin lit another cigarette.

'Good, well, you passed the test this time. Well done. Every test you take will take you one step further down your path, one step nearer to the Palace and away from the Abyss, and away from a world of eternal pain.'

I nodded, trying to take it all in. Of course I wanted to go to the Palace, to be with the Gods. I didn't want to end up in the Abyss. Still, I felt in quite a lot of pain right at this minute.

'I want you to succeed in the Church,' Colin went on. 'I want you to do well and, as long as you want the same for yourself, as long as you choose to follow your path, you will achieve astonishing things, Anna. You will become a Priestess, a Goddess. Like I said, the Gods have chosen you; they are watching you all the time. Make sure you follow your path.'

I didn't feel like a Goddess at that moment – I felt dirty, ashamed and cold – but I dared not pull my clothes back on without Colin saying I could. Finally he noticed I was shivering.

He pulled his trousers up and said: 'OK, you better go and get some sleep now. I've got to put some more of this wallpaper up.'

I crawled into bed and, despite the pain, fell asleep almost immediately. When I woke the next day I was still very sore down below. I hobbled out onto the landing to see that there was still just the one sheet of new wallpaper on the wall.

For the next eight weeks Colin came into our house nightly and, while he decorated our house at an almost catatonic rate, he put me through dozens of tests. Funnily enough, Mum was always round at his house playing PlayStation in the evenings and my sister was in bed asleep. Dark circles began to form round my eyes. I was always sleepy now from my broken nights. During the day I was a normal little girl – jumping on the bouncy castle, talking to the other kids in our Church, playing with Hope's Barbies – but at night I was Colin's, and it was always the same: me lying back on the bed, and him doing stuff to me.

It was inevitable, then, that I changed over that summer. On the surface you might not have noticed much but I definitely knew I wasn't the same inside. Something was missing. I wasn't carefree any more – I didn't laugh easily or naturally. Much of the time I was faking it, putting on a front so nobody would know that I walked around with my stomach in knots, full of dread and anxiety. By the time I started senior school in September I was a very different person, though nobody knew the truth of what I was going through. And funnily enough, he never did finish decorating the house.

Chapter 6

School

'Have you got any money today, Annabelle?'

It was the support teacher, Miss Burns, who stopped me in the corridor that breaktime. Miss Burns was young; she had a kind face and small crinkly eyes framed by a mop of red curly hair. She was the only teacher I truly respected and the only one who could get me to settle down and concentrate in class.

'No, Miss,' I replied.

'Come here then.' She rooted around in her tartan fabric purse. 'Here you go – there's 30p for toast.'

'Thanks, Miss.' I smiled back. It wasn't the first time this week she'd given me money. Thirty pence bought two slices of toast from our school canteen – it was just what I needed to stop the dull ache of hunger that seemed to follow me everywhere. There was never much for breakfast in our house, so I often went to school without eating and I didn't get pocket money either. Colin had taken over giving me lunch money from my mum, but quite often he forgot. Consequently I was skinny as a rake and hunger was just a normal part of my life.

It was Miss Burns who noticed how thin I was and that I never seemed to have any money for the canteen. She was a sweet woman, full of generosity and concern. Better than my own mum really. I don't think Mum would have cared if I'd starved – she just couldn't be bothered any more. My uniform was paid for with a school grant and although she washed the black trousers, white shirt and navy jumper I wore for school, it was up to me to iron my own clothes and get myself to the school bus every day. After a while she stopped doing the washing too. But I didn't mind. Nothing was going to stop me going to school.

I loved it. Admittedly, the first few weeks had been a bit scary – it was so much bigger than my primary school. But I already knew a fair number of the other children in my class, as we'd come up together and it didn't take long to make new friends. In fact, school was the one place I could truly be myself. Hope was in the year above and, together, away from Colin's watchful gaze, we could relax and enjoy ourselves. She was his princess, of course, but he was as strict with her as he was with the rest of us – even she had to put her hand up if she wanted to speak to him.

At school, away from Colin and the Church rules, we were free. So we mucked around together and, for the most part, I didn't pay much attention to my lessons. In class I talked, joked, talked back to the teachers, and failed to hand in my homework. I enjoyed being a kid again, just being me. I wasn't so naughty that I got into real trouble but I gave the teachers a hard time and they didn't expect much from me in terms of grades.

It didn't matter – my mum didn't give a toss about my

education. When I handed her my report card to sign she'd just throw it on the kitchen counter, barely giving it a look. She never helped me with my homework and didn't bother turning up to parents' evenings to hear how I was flunking every subject. No, Mum didn't care about anyone but Colin. Meanwhile, as the school year progressed, Colin kept up with the tests on me until they started to blend into our everyday life. I didn't even see them as tests any more – it felt like a normal part of my life now, just like hunger.

It could happen anywhere and at any time of the day or night. I could be playing in his living room with Hope and he'd fix me with one of his hard stares and say: 'You. I want a word with you.' Then I'd have to follow him to his room for sex.

He never seemed to show any concern that someone might discover us because everyone did what Colin said. If he closed the door, that door stayed closed. He had absolute power over his home, the cul-de-sac and everyone in our Church. Sometimes he'd tell me he was coming round to the house to see me later and that meant I'd have to wait up for him in the living room. On a good night he would come round before midnight – on a bad night I'd be up waiting for him until 3 a.m. Mum must have known what was going on at this point – if she was going to bed herself I had to say I was waiting for Colin, so I imagine she knew what he was coming round for.

The late nights, Colin's demands on me – it meant I found it hard to concentrate in lessons. Miss Burns did her best – she had a way of giving out soft but firm instructions that made me settle down and stop disturbing the other children. It wasn't that I couldn't *do* the work; it was just that I had so much on my mind I couldn't focus. And school was the one place I could go to talk to other people, to find out what other people thought and did with their time. It was far more interesting than anything I read in a book.

By the end of the day, I'd always start to worry about going home, about what Colin might have planned for me that night or whether my mum would be in a bad mood, as usual, or a *really* bad mood, where she would snap and shout at us if we dared to try and speak to her. She never smiled at us – only at Colin.

By now I was scared of my mum, not because she was strict with me – she didn't care enough to get upset over anything I said or did. It was always Colin that disciplined me, never her. No, it was more the fact that she was distant, unreachable. I never knew what she was thinking or feeling and that made her unpredictable. Like a dormant volcano, her hostility towards me was always simmering below the surface, ready to explode at any moment.

The only time I could truly forget about my home life and all my anxiety melted away was when I was doing cross-country running. Out in the woodlands, behind the hockey pitch where we'd do our training, I'd pound round and round until every muscle in my body ached. Out there, surrounded by the damp, musty trees, I was in control again – it was my body and I could do what I liked with it. I felt my heart thump, heard the leaves and twigs crunch under my feet and the wind lashed at my limbs and I felt free. Truly free.

Netball too, helped me forget about what waited for me back at home. When I got stuck into a game of netball everything else in the world disappeared. Small and athletic, I was made wing attack, which meant I was almost always in a position to get the ball. So from the moment the whistle blew, I was on the go, darting left and right, spinning, jumping, passing, blocking, ducking or shooting. It was as if, for that hour, nothing else mattered. I was totally focused on the players around me, my teammates and scoring goals. It wasn't so much that I was competitive or wanted to beat another team, I just relished the opportunity to lose myself in the moment.

Sport was the one thing I felt I was good at, so I threw myself into it. Besides anything else, it gave me a real confidence boost to excel at something. So it didn't take long for me to get picked for the school netball and athletics teams. There, at the tournaments, I felt normal again, just like all the other girls. I practically flew around the netball court in my white Aertex top, shorts and trainers. I loved it so much, so it was frustrating when I had to tell my PE teacher I couldn't come to after-school practice.

'You'll be dropped from the team if you don't come,' she warned.

I shrugged. 'My mum hasn't got a car – she can't pick me up.'

This was a lie. I wasn't *allowed* to tell her the truth – that the Church banned after-school activities. It was against the rules: just like going to the park, the shop, the cinema or a friend's house. I had to be home with the school bus or I'd get the slipper.

'Isn't there someone else who can pick you up?' the PE teacher doing her best to keep me in the team, but I shook my head and walked away, simmering with frustration. Of course I wanted to go to after-school practice! All the families in the Church had a car, so any of them could have collected me. It just wasn't allowed, and that was all there was to it. The horrible thing was Mum didn't even know I was good at netball or running. She didn't care, she didn't ask and I didn't say.

Inevitably, after my first year, I was dropped from the school's first netball team, though I could take part when the games were played within school hours. On one occasion there was a county-wide athletics competition at Pembrey beach. I was picked to compete in the cross-country race and, on a crystal-clear December day, I ran for two hours non-stop and came 28th out of 200 kids in the county. It didn't matter to me that I had done well – I had loved every moment. The ice-cold salty spray stung at my cheeks, as I pumped my arms in time with my step. Out on the beach, looking at the wide sandy horizon, I felt on top of the world. I lengthened my stride, pushing myself harder and harder, and though the pain in my thighs throbbed with every pace, I did something I rarely did at home. I smiled.

It wasn't long after I started secondary school that the meetings began. All the Church members, including the children, had to congregate at Colin's house at noon on Sunday to read from our Church's version of the Bible – *The Book of The Law*. I didn't know exactly where this book came from at the time. Colin told us that we were Mormons, but I realize now that this was just a cover in case anyone asked us to name our religion. After all, everyone has heard of the Mormons – they seem innocent and well-meaning with their clean-shaven men, crisp white shirts and wide smiles. But I found out later our Church shared very little in common with Mormonism.

On the surface it might have seemed similar – we had strict health laws about not drinking alcohol, swearing or abusing drugs. But underneath it was chalk and cheese. Mormons followed strict laws of chastity – our religion actively despised chastity. A line in *The Book of The Law* actually says: 'Let all chaste women be despised.'

Years later, I discovered that *The Book of The Law* was written in the 19th century by a man called Aleister Crowley. Crowley was into group sex, sadomasochism, drugs and ancient mysticism. No wonder he told everyone to do what they wanted. He certainly didn't hold back himself. In fact, there are people who still follow his teachings today, called Thelemites. Not that I knew anything like that as a child.

At twelve years old I knew nothing except what Colin and my school taught me. Since we didn't even own a computer I didn't know that I could look up the answers to these things. Every Sunday all seventeen members of our Church would gather in Colin's living room and we would take it in turns to read aloud from *The Book of The Law*. One person read while the rest of us listened. The entire text is divided into three books and each one took around forty-five minutes to read out loud. I guess it wouldn't have mattered so much but for the fact that the thing was completely incomprehensible. At the time I just thought I was stupid for not understanding but, looking back at those verses, I'm amazed so many adults took it so seriously.

After the reading we would be allowed to ask Colin questions about what we had just heard. Most of the adults were very keen on this part and they'd put their hands up to ask him to clarify what certain verses meant. Then Colin would ramble on and on, talking about the Gods, the meaning of the words, the Church, the Palace and anything else that came up. As a result, the meetings often went on until 7 p.m. in the evening with no breaks and no food or drink allowed. It was excruciating for us kids.

We were made to memorize whole chunks of text from *The Book of The Law*, and even today I can remember the opening passage: '*Had! The manifestation of Nuit. The unveiling of the company of heaven. Every man and every woman is a star. Every number is infinite, there is no difference.*'

I remember Colin explained in a meeting once that this meant everyone in our Church was equal – we were all stars and there was no difference between us. But of course we were different! Every single one of us was ranked within the Church and the order of importance was clear from the beginning. Colin was at the top, followed by Elaine, then Mum, Sandra, Shelley and so on. Colin himself talked about our paths and how we should all be trying to climb higher in the Church. He ranked himself as the Prince Priest, so I don't see how he truly believed we were all the same.

Occasionally a question would come up which Colin refused to answer. He'd trot out the old line that the information was 'governed under Church secrecy'. There were lots of things that were governed in this way, it seemed, although Colin never explained why some things were secret and other things weren't.

According to him, we were only one part of the Church, which had chapters all over the country.

'We are bigger than any of you realize,' Colin would tell us. 'When you're walking down the street, you are passing other Church members. You don't know it but we are around you all the time. We are everywhere.'

The way he spoke, always saying 'we', it was like he *was* the Church. Famous people too were members, he said, and I was always dying for him to tell us but he wouldn't because it was all 'governed under Church secrecy'.

I suppose the meetings were just one aspect of the Church we had to endure, like other kids were made to go to Sunday School or Quran lessons, but there were times I really hated being there. The worst bit was when Colin picked on someone in the group. Just the fear of this was enough to keep me in line. If one of the kids had done something wrong that week, Colin would tell them off in front of everyone at the meeting. Often it was one of his own sons – he didn't seem to like them very much. While he was delightful to Hope, he was pretty rotten to his sons and he was always calling them names and embarrassing them – telling everyone they were 'gay' or 'dirty'.

These ritual humiliations were perhaps my most dreaded moments. Being in Colin's bad books was frightening. It meant you wouldn't progress in the Church, that you would never make it to the Palace. I tried to make sense of it all as best I could, but a lot of the verses from *The Book of The Law* just went in one ear and out the other. The words didn't mean anything to me. The one thing I knew for certain was that I didn't want to go to the Abyss. I didn't want to suffer an eternity of pain, so I tried to be a good girl, to follow the rules and secure my place in the Palace.

By Monday morning I was back at school and no one there knew anything about the Church, the tests or *The Book*. I never told a soul about anything that went on at home. So home was home, school was school, and I just tried to be good and follow my path, knowing that the Gods were watching me all the time.

Chapter 7

No Such Thing as a Mother

I was burning up. Underneath the hood of my blue silken robe droplets of sweat trickled down the side of my neck and fell onto my bare back.

Urgh, when will this end?

It was a special day today – one of our thanksgiving ceremonies. Once every few months we gave thanks to the Gods and wore our ceremonial robes for the occasion. These were full-length gowns with hoods. The colour of your gown depended on your rank within the Church. Most of the children had light-blue ones like me, but the adults tended to wear dark-purple gowns.

We stood facing the wall with the Egyptian pictures, in rows, fanning out like a pyramid. Colin stood at the front, then behind him was my mum and Elaine, three more in the row behind them, then four and so on. Colin presided over a table covered by a purple sheet which held silver candlesticks, a silver goblet of red wine and a silver plate with brown bread soaked in wine. Everyone was silent while Colin read from one of our sacred texts and then we took it in turns to go to the front for a sip of wine and a small piece of bread.

I'd already been up to receive my bread and wine, which as usual, tasted disgusting, and I'd returned to my place in the third row of the pyramid, but now I began to sway slightly as the heat started to get to me. The air was thick and heavy with bitter incense, the windows closed and the curtains drawn. Meanwhile, all three bars were turned up on the electric heater next to where I was standing. It was May outside – a beautiful sunny spring day with a breeze that rippled through the trees and made the flower heads bob. But you wouldn't know it here. Inside, the air was stifling. I longed to be outside, running in the open air. I was naked underneath the gown – we all were, that was one of the rules – but even so, I was so hot I could barely breathe. Somewhere far off I heard Colin's voice rumble on but now I felt I was floating away and I could barely stay on my feet. The next thing, I felt a hand on my arm, pulling me out of line and then someone, firmly gripping my shoulders from behind, guided me out of the room. My eyes were half closed and I didn't know who it was steering me towards the corridor.

Dazed, I was plonked on the staircase and left to recover as I watched the purple robe sweep back into the living room. Whoever it was, I was grateful for the fresh air. Out in the corridor I could breathe again and, slowly, my head started to clear from the dense fog which seemed to have clogged up my brain. I don't know how long I was sat there before the door opened again and I caught a waft of incense. Slowly, Church members began to appear. They had to exit line by line, starting with the last row, but without turning their backs to the pictures, so that when they came out you could only see the gowns from behind, not the faces of the people inside them. One by one these faceless robes swished past me and then went through to the kitchen to get changed into their normal clothes. Nobody spoke to me or even looked in my direction. Sitting there on my own, I felt stupid and embarrassed.

Since I didn't know what I was supposed to be doing, I stayed where I'd been put – on the step. Finally, the last purple gown emerged. It was Colin. He came straight up to speak to me.

'You were going to faint,' he said, kneeling down and pushing back his hood to reveal his long black hair, speckled with grey strands. He wasn't too happy with me. 'I saw you rocking back and forth and your eyes were half closed. I had to take you out of there myself.'

'I'm sorry, Colin.' I felt ashamed of myself. It was a really bad thing to miss a ceremony like this. I knew they were very important in the development of our paths.

'You've *got* to be able to deal with the heat,' he admonished. 'It's no good like this, having to take you out in the middle of the events. It's disruptive to everyone, but especially to yourself. You're going to find it very difficult to progress any further in the Church if you can't get through a thanksgiving ceremony. This is an important day – and you could have ruined it. OK, now go and get changed. Next time, you have to do better.'

I felt terrible for the rest of the day. How come I couldn't make it through the ceremony? It was only a couple of hours long. I'd never been good dealing with heat but then, it wasn't like I was even wearing that much. Suddenly I felt a gnawing hunger claw at my insides. I was starving. Lunch was a simple cheese sandwich – I made one for myself and one for Olivia because Mum had disappeared after the meeting.

Pushing back my chair afterwards, I definitely felt better. Perhaps that's why I'd nearly fainted. I'd only had a Pot Noodle the night before and there was nothing for breakfast this morning. In my home economics class I recalled the teacher saying it was important to eat regularly in order to keep your energy levels up, something to do with blood sugar. Perhaps not eating was becoming a problem. I decided that next time there was a meeting I would try to eat something before going in, even if it was just a piece of fruit. The thought of jeopardizing my future in the Church was really scary. After all, I knew that I couldn't miss any of the ceremonies if I wanted to improve my path. And with all the tests I'd been doing, it felt so silly to let myself down in this way.

Now fourteen, I was truly a committed member of the Church. Colin had given me many tests over the years and he had begun to teach me the ways of the Scarlet Woman too. According to Colin, the Scarlet Woman was the wife of the Prince Priest and together they were given the power to bring the glory of the stars into the hearts of man. *The Book of The Law* taught us about the Scarlet Woman and what was expected of her. He said it could be me, the one the Gods would choose, to bring together the division of man and woman.

But I had to prove myself, prove my commitment to the joys of ecstasy, and the truth of revelation. I had to prove that I was willing to give myself over completely to our Church and to make my body a conduit for the True Will to flow through. Colin told us that really, there was no such thing as family within our Church since we were all governed under the sacred powers of the Gods.

'There is no such thing as mother or father here,' he said. 'We don't have brothers or sisters. We are all stars – we are all one and we are all none. There is only will, love under will.'

When Colin spoke it sounded so powerful and impressive. The way he could quote whole chunks of *The Book of The Law* or speak in Egyptian, it was amazing really. Over the years I'd really come to see him as my leader in a lot of ways, and I did try my best to fulfil all my duties within the Church. But the idea that there was no such thing as family was a very difficult one to get my head around. I couldn't help feeling that my mum was still my mum and my sister was my sister. Colin said this was an issue I had to address. So after I turned fourteen he directed my tests in this area by involving my mum.

'Colin's coming round tonight,' Mum said before I left for school that day. I was distracted because I had a maths test that morning and I hadn't had a chance to revise all weekend.

Now I paid little attention to what she was saying because I was desperately scanning the house for my book bag, which I hadn't touched for three days and could very well be anywhere at this point.

'What?' I replied, not really listening.

'Colin's coming round tonight, after school. He wants to see both of us. Got it?'

'Yeah, OK,' I mumbled, biting my nails. It was fairly normal for Colin to come round to see one of us and it didn't really strike me as anything unusual when Mum mentioned it. I hardly thought about it all day, in fact, as I struggled through a difficult maths test. My teacher sighed heavily as I handed in my work that morning. It was a clear flunk – I hadn't even managed to fill up a whole page of A4. Everyone else handed in reams of paper. I could barely understand the questions.

The previous week I'd been pulled into the staff room for yet another 'little chat' with my form teacher – she was worried I wouldn't get any GCSEs.

'At this rate, Annabelle, you won't make it through to year eleven.' She had locked my eyes with hers and, though I squirmed with discomfort, I knew she had a good point.

'I'm genuinely very concerned. There has to be a change of attitude on your part. The way things are going you won't be getting any qualifications at all.'

'I'll try harder, Miss,' I'd promised. And I meant it at the time; I wanted to do better at school. I had hopes of going to college one day. I didn't want to just sit around the house watching TV like my mum and some of the other women in the Church. I wanted a job, a career – I felt if I worked hard enough I could do something with my life. The trouble was, I found it so difficult to work at home, and in school I was constantly distracted.

'You've got to demonstrate something a little more committed than "trying harder", Annabelle,' said Miss Green. 'We need to see results. You've got this term to turn things around.

If I don't see any real improvement then we'll have to discuss other options.'

At the time I felt that was the moment I would start to try harder but now, a few days later, I could see that I'd already let myself down again. It felt so frustrating that while I'd passed every test Colin set me, I didn't do half as well for those at school. I really wanted to sit my exams with everyone else, so I spent the rest of the day concentrating hard in every lesson. I wasn't stupid, and I didn't want to get left behind my classmates – I knew it was mostly a matter of improving my concentration.

That night, as soon as tea was over, I went upstairs and did all of my homework in one go. In fact, my mind was so occupied with my work for a change, that it came as a surprise when Mum poked her head round the door and ordered me to come into the living room with her, after she'd put Olivia to bed that night. Olivia usually got to stay up a little later than 8 p.m. so she huffed off to her room, stomping up the stairs pointedly.

I'd completely forgotten about Colin coming over and now I followed her into the lounge, absent-mindedly, not really noticing that she'd got changed in to her silky dressing gown. I was still in my school uniform.

'Here,' she said, handing me my own fluffy blue towelling robe. 'Put this on.'

I went upstairs and changed in the bathroom and, when I came back downstairs, she had taken all the cushions off the sofa and laid them out on the floor, covered by a large red sheet.

'What you wearing underneath?' she asked, as I sat on the cushion-less sofa.

'My underwear,' I told her.

'Well, take it off,' she snapped, so I tramped back upstairs to take my knickers and bra off. When I got back downstairs Mum had closed the curtains and was perched on the edge of the sofa, her elbows on her knees and her hands linked together around a lit cigarette. She smoked impatiently, picking at her cuticles between drags. I sat down next to her, to wait, and she flicked on the TV so we could watch *EastEnders*.

Half an hour later we heard the back door slam – Colin had arrived. I didn't know what to expect on this occasion. I'd never sat down here with my mum before but I knew this must be another test.

Colin was smoking when he walked in – he didn't say anything at first, he just laid himself down on the cushions on the floor.

My mum's whole body seemed to react to his presence – her back lengthened, her spine grew straighter and her chest came forward. Suddenly she flicked her long dark hair over to one side and puckered her lips. I sat there, waiting for whatever came next.

Colin leaned back on one elbow, casting his eyes around the room: 'Right, well, have you got any questions?'

I shook my head. I didn't know what the hell was going on but I figured I'd soon find out.

'It's about the Three Ordeals,' Mum began. She usually had a few questions. 'I know that the first two are fire and intellect, but I don't really understand what the third one is.'

'Yes, the highest ordeal.' Colin nodded and put a hand through his wiry hair to push it off his face. 'I'm afraid this isn't an area I can discuss openly since it's governed under Church secrecy. The first two ordeals must be achieved before it's possible to learn the third. One must achieve the higher level of spiritual awareness to make this discovery. Now, requests?'

I'd never been asked if I had a request before, so I just shook my head but Mum was obviously not new to this because she was ready with her list: 'I need to get Olivia new shoes and the cat needs a new litter tray.'

We had recently got a Siamese cat called Sakkara – she was beautiful, pure black ears fading into a creamy white coat with amazing blue eyes. Sadly she'd come from a bad home and, at first, we couldn't get near her. In the past few months, however, she'd settled down a little and occasionally let us stroke her if she thought it would get her some food. Colin had brought her to us and I knew he wanted to breed from her, but at the moment she was still easily spooked. When she got left in the house on her own she destroyed her litter tray.

Colin acknowledged Mum's requests with a tiny nod of the head and then he said something inaudible. But Mum obviously understood because, next thing, she slipped off her robe and was naked underneath. It was weird, seeing her naked like this. I hadn't seen my mum without her clothes on before, only that once when I caught her doing her meditation. Up close like this, I saw all the little lines and crevices in her skin, the tiny moles on the inside of her thigh. It felt strange.

She knelt down beside Colin and started easing his tracksuit bottoms down over his hips. From where I was sitting it looked like there was a little tussle because she wanted to take them off completely but Colin wasn't letting her. She was trying to yank them over his feet but he was moving his legs around to stop her. From somewhere deep inside me I felt a desperate giggle build up and threaten to erupt. I was nervous, uncomfortable, and now they were having a bizarre fight over Colin's tracksuit bottoms. God, I hated this. Whatever was going to happen, I just wanted it to be over as soon as possible. Finally, with the tracksuit bottoms still around his ankles, Colin said to Mum: 'That'll do.'

Now she started to give him oral sex. I just sat watching her do this to him. It really was only a matter of time before he turned to me and gestured for me to come over. I guessed I had to get involved somehow, so I took my robe off as well and then knelt on the other side of him.

She looked up briefly and murmured, 'Lick his balls.' Then she went back to giving him oral sex. It was another test, one more ordeal I had to go through. So I did as she told me and later he pulled her on top of him and I had to kiss him at the same time. After that we swapped. Mum was making all these noises, like she was enjoying herself. Me, I didn't make a sound. I didn't feel as if I was really there. It was all too strange to cope with – I let myself do these things but really my mind was somewhere else. After a good half an hour it all came to an end and Colin left. Then I was allowed to go upstairs to my bedroom to finish my homework.

I'd like to say that I felt awful after this but I guess I didn't. I didn't really feel anything at all. I was there in body only. I did what I had to do because I didn't have any choice in the matter. From this point, sex with both of them became a regular fixture in my life. Just another adjustment I had to make – there was sex with Colin every couple of days and this once a week.

Thinking about it now, it's hard to believe I just put up with it as normal, but I didn't know any different and I wasn't allowed to think it was wrong. In fact, Colin always went out of his way to remind us both that there was no such thing as family and no such thing as a mother-daughter bond. And I suppose in some ways it was bearable. I could put up with it while we were just meant to be pleasuring Colin. It's what came next that I found sickening.

About two months after the first time with my mum and Colin, we were preparing for him to come round. We'd put the sofa cushions on the floor as usual and were just sat waiting in our dressing gowns when my mum turned to me and said I needed to relax more during sex.

'You're too uptight,' she said. 'Tonight, before he comes round, Colin wants me to give you oral sex.'

I froze. I knew I didn't want her to do this but I didn't have any choice. The Gods were watching us all the time, and if I refused to do as she asked she would tell Colin and then I'd be punished.

She told me to lie down on the floor and that's when she did it to me. I can't begin to describe how terrible I felt that whole time. Sickened, I hated every second. I wanted to jump up and run out of there but I was too scared to move and some part of my brain actually shut down at that point. It was as if it was happening to someone else. Even thinking about it now makes me feel ill. Of all the terrible things my mum did to me through the years, this was surely the worst. It was wrong – I knew it was wrong then – but I didn't know how to stop it.

Sometime later, Colin came round and when he walked in to the living room he was wearing a knowing smirk. He looked at us both sitting there on the sofa as we always did, but this time my cheeks burned with humiliation and horror. He looked straight at me, his dark eyes dancing with delight behind his thick spectacles.

'Well, Annabelle,' he said. 'Did you enjoy that tonight?'

'Yes,' I replied quietly.

That's what I said to him – yes, I enjoyed it. Well, that's what was expected of me, so that's what I said. He didn't know the truth – that it was the worst experience of my life. That the awfulness of it had sent me to a place inside myself I didn't even know existed. Whoever I'd been before was gone, lost completely. Inside, I felt dead.

Chapter 8

Thomas

'Is there something you want to ask me?' Mum turned to look directly at me. Her hand hovered in mid-air, the blade of the kitchen knife glinted in the sunlight.

She stood at the kitchen drawer, sorting out knives, while I munched slowly on my sandwich. I guess she must have caught me looking at her funny. It was her stomach I was staring at – in the sunshine her slim profile revealed a large bump just over her pelvis.

I couldn't help it, I had to know.

'Yeah, are you pregnant?'

'Yeah, I am,' she replied matter-of-factly and then turned back to her job at the cutlery drawer. I didn't say anything else – I didn't know what else to say.

I was still fourteen and my sister was now nine years old, so it seemed a little odd that my mum was going to have another baby. But still, I was pleased. I liked babies and I was quite excited that we would be having one in our house. Word quickly spread among the Church that she was pregnant. It was Colin's

— I knew that for a fact because I was there when they'd had sex without a condom. But since all the tests were governed under Church secrecy nobody else knew.

Almost immediately the rumour sprang up that Alan had come back for a night and the baby was his. When I heard this from one of the other girls, I raised my eyebrows and said, 'Oh yeah,' as if I believed that too. But I knew this was rubbish, probably made up by Colin to stop Elaine thinking he was the dad. We hadn't seen Alan in years.

By now Colin had bought a caravan in Tenby for the family, so he'd often send Elaine and Hope up there at the weekends for a little break. He usually stayed behind to look after the house and the dogs – it meant he could get on with what he wanted to do without Elaine knowing anything about it.

By this time I'd guessed he was having sex with some of the other girls too – Fiona and Millie were always round Colin's house and he would mess around with them when Elaine was away at the caravan. He thought it was funny to lift up Millie's top whenever he walked past her, to expose her boobs. Everyone laughed when he did this, except me. I didn't think it was funny; I lived in fear that he might try and do this to me one day, so I always kept away from him when we were around other people. Millie would stay over at his place whenever Elaine and Hope were away; she became a little bit like his second wife. I didn't mind – anything that kept Colin away from me was a good thing.

One week there was a new rule: all us girls had to wear skirts whenever Elaine was up in Tenby. The next week the rule was made more specific: the skirts had to be short. And the week after that another new rule: we all had to wear make-up like Egyptian goddesses. So all the girls and women, including Shelley and Sandra, would put on teeny little skirts and draw dramatic black lines around their eyes to replicate the 'Cleopatra' look, at the weekends.

It pleased Colin hugely – he said it was the way of the Scarlet Woman, and we had to show our devotion to him and to the Church by trying to make ourselves look the right way for him. By now all the girls were competing against each other for Colin's affection and attention. Me, I didn't want to look attractive for Colin but I still had to follow the rules, so I wore a short skirt and did my make-up just as he asked. The fact was I wasn't interested in competing for his attention. I didn't want him anywhere near me. But he had become more demanding in the bedroom recently.

Now, he didn't just do it lying down; he put me in all different positions and he insisted that I look at him during sex. He seemed to be enjoying himself more, getting more passionate and kissing me lots, which was horrible. He'd push his tongue round and round inside and on top of my mouth for ages, making the skin around my lips all wet, which then got sore afterwards. Sometimes he'd try to pleasure me but I felt nothing, so I just faked it, pretending I was having a good time just to get it over with.

Now, during sex, he'd bite me with his one big tooth. It was painful, proper biting – but he wanted that. Colin often told me he wanted me to take the pain because I had to learn to endure. Part of being the Scarlet Woman meant enduring the Three Ordeals. So he did it and it hurt but I never cried. I never ever cried any more. The next day I'd have to wear a scarf at school to cover the bruises and bite marks he left on my neck.

It wasn't long after I found out about Mum's pregnancy that Colin called me into the kitchen for a 'word'. Earlier that day I'd been round at his house and Orla's son, Thomas, had been there too.

'You fancy her, don't you?' he'd teased, pointing at me.

Trying to hide his embarrassment, Thomas had mumbled: 'Oh please!'

'Well, you do, don't you?'

'Yeah, of course,' Thomas had said, like I wasn't even there. 'She's fit. She's got a nice face and stuff.'

'There you go, Annabelle. I've found you a boyfriend. How d'you fancy going out with Thomas, then?'

I'd been so mortified by all of this I'd barely said a word of reply. The conversation soon moved on and I'd returned home an hour later, barely thinking about this humiliating encounter. It was Colin's speciality – he loved making others feel uncomfortable. But now it seemed he had a plan.

'Right, tonight I want you to go round to Shelley's place and have sex with Thomas,' he said. Thomas was five years older than me. He was a nice enough lad – tall and thin with a shaved head and thick eyebrows that met in the middle – but I didn't want to have sex with him. I didn't want to have sex with *anybody* and I didn't understand why Colin was making me do this now.

I bit down hard on my lip and said: 'I really don't want to.'

'No, I *want* you to do it,' he smiled crookedly, exposing his one big tooth. 'You're my special girl and I want you to do it.'

I was fourteen and Thomas nineteen when I was sent over to sleep with him for the first time. He lived in Shelley's house because he wanted to be near the rest of the Church, especially Colin. Thomas was a committed member of the Church and went to all the meetings and ceremonies. During the day he worked stacking shelves in Asda and, like every other Church member, he gave his wages to Colin. The first time I went round to his small room for sex was a pretty grim affair. I was still trying to make an effort with my school work, so I made sure I finished my home-work first, and I wasn't at his until about 9 p.m.

Shelley let me in the house and showed me straight up to his room – she obviously knew what I was doing there. I pushed open the door and he was already in bed, naked from the waist up. Thomas and I didn't know each other that well, so neither of us knew what to say to each other. Looking at him now, all ready, I guessed we just had to get on with it. Turning my back to him, I undressed quickly, pulling down my black school trou-sers and slipping my white shirt and navy jumper over my head, then jumped into the bed next to him. His skin felt cold and rough next to mine – I lay there and let him put his large hands on me. I could hear him breathing hard now, as he explored my body in the dark.

Please, just let this be over quickly.

I lay there and waited while he got on with it. By now, I had learnt how to make myself absent at the moment of sex, and although I knew somewhere that he was heaving himself on top of me, slipping himself between my legs, in actual fact I was miles away.

My mind wandered back to the fields and the woods I ran through when I was doing cross-country. I felt my body being moved around but it was far away from me now. I was pounding through the leafy tracks, the earthy smell of the trees filling my nostrils, my arms swinging lightly by my sides, my legs working hard but taking the ground lightly. On and on I ran – now I was on the beach, tasting the salty air on my lips, feeling my hair whip my cheeks as the foamy white waves broke over the horizon. I squinted into the sunlight, dipping down behind the dunes, and felt the spray of seawater on my shins as each foot landed along the shore. The gulls screamed overhead . . .

'Are you OK?'

Suddenly it was dark and I heard Thomas's voice as if from far away.

'What?' I felt confused as the sunlight fled and I found myself lying naked on his bed. Thomas was next to me, his head resting on one elbow, a concerned look on his face.

'Are you all right? You've been lying there like that for ages. Do you want something? A drink maybe? I'm going to the kitchen.'

'No.' I turned on my side, away from him. 'I'm all right. I'm just tired, that's all. Good night.'

I closed my eyes again and let sleep take me. It was over, thank God, and now I could relax. Funnily enough, I fell straight to sleep and stayed that way, all night long. But the next morning I felt awkward and self-conscious, trying to get ready in a new place with Thomas watching me from the bed. It was really early and I wanted to be gone before the others woke but, as I went to the door, Thomas grabbed my arm and pulled me back to the bed, trying to land a kiss on my mouth. I was so surprised I didn't know how to react. Instinctively, I turned my mouth away and his lips grazed my cheeks, embarrassing us both. In another minute, I was down the stairs and out of the house, relieved to be on my own again.

Waiting for the bus that morning, I couldn't help wondering what this was all about. It seemed he really thought I wanted to be there; he'd smiled at me a lot and had tried to kiss me in bed that morning.

Does he think we're in a relationship? I wondered. *Doesn't he realize I'm being made to do this for the Church? For Colin!*

I really hoped I didn't have to do this again – I had enough on my plate as it was. On the other hand, I'd slept really well. At least in Shelley's house I was free from worrying about my mum and Colin.

Later that evening, Colin came to our house while I watched TV with Olivia. I didn't spend much time with Hope any more. Ever since Mum had got pregnant she'd been really off with me. It hurt – after all, she'd been my best friend for years now and I missed her badly. I knew that she and Elaine suspected Colin was the father of the baby but that wasn't *my* fault. How could she punish me like this? I desperately wanted to talk to her about it all. I wanted to tell her the things I was going through but I couldn't even begin to start that conversation.

What could I say? *Yes, Hope, it's true your dad is having sex with my mum and, while we're at it, he's been having sex with me too for the past three years!* It just wasn't going to happen. Meanwhile, Elaine had also stopped inviting us round, so these days me, Mum and Olivia spent most of the time at home together. It was lonely, but at least this way I'd been able to focus more on my studies and my grades were beginning to reflect this.

From the hallway Colin gestured for me to 'come here' with his finger, and I slid off the sofa and went to talk to him in the kitchen.

'So, did you enjoy it?' he asked. I knew he was talking about my night with Thomas.

'Not really,' I replied sullenly.

'Got a bigger dick than me, has he?'

'No,' I replied, casting my eyes downwards. I didn't want to be having this conversation. A long silence fell between us.

Then: 'Well, how do you fancy going back there tomorrow night?'

I shrugged. It didn't bother me any more, nothing really bothered me.

'Oh, so you *want* to have sex with him, do you?' Colin leered. I knew what he wanted. He wanted resistance. He wanted me to object so that he could show me he had the power to make me do it. I realized then that it didn't matter what I said or did. He would always win – so, as usual, I gave him what he wanted.

'No, I don't want to have sex with him.'

'No – you only want to have sex with me, don't you!' he grinned triumphantly. 'Well, be a good girl for me now. I want you round to his again tomorrow. Now get upstairs and lie down.'

And that was how Colin engineered a supposedly 'normal' relationship between me and Orla's son Thomas. Nobody knew, least of all Thomas himself, that I was being forced into having sex with him.

And still nobody knew that I was also having regular sex with Colin and with my mum and Colin at the same time. From the outside, and to everyone in our small community, it looked like Thomas and I were now boyfriend and girlfriend. The truth was that Thomas could only have me if he got Colin's permission.

He had to ask Colin first – which was always horrible for me because he'd do it right in front of everyone, without even asking me first.

'Can Annabelle stay at mine tonight?' he'd beg, like a child asking to stay up beyond bedtime. Colin would always smile and laugh – he loved manipulating all of us like this. For my part, I felt like a piece of meat being passed from one person to the next. I didn't have a say or choice in the matter and, in truth, I felt less and less like a proper human being. Inside I was cold, dead to the world. I never laughed or cried at all. It was like I was made of stone.

Even Thomas noticed that I never seemed to be affectionate with him and, one day, a few months after our so-called relationship began, he tried to end things. He didn't tell me, of course, he told Colin.

Colin came into our house one evening and pulled me up to my room, a dark and dreadful look on his face.

'What's going on with you?' he snarled, pushing me back onto my bed.

'What do you mean?'

'You're failing me, Anna, and you're failing the Church.'

My blood went cold at that moment and I started to shake. The thought of failing the Church was terrifying – it was all I had to stop myself from being swallowed by the Abyss.

'I don't know what you mean.' I tried to rack my brains to think of all the things I'd done recently. *What was it?*

'I've just had Thomas round my place and he's not happy,' Colin thundered, towering over me. 'He wants to finish things with you. He says you don't seem to like him very much – you don't talk to him, don't kiss him. I mean, what are you doing round there? You've got to be nicer to him. You've got to act more normally. Be nice, kiss him. Talk to him. He thinks you don't care.'

Colin was ranting now, pacing back and forth, and I sat there, unable to speak. I wanted to tell the truth – I *didn't* care. I didn't *want* to be in a relationship with him – but of course it wasn't about what *I* wanted. I had to do my duty and be nice to Thomas. Not too nice, though, otherwise Colin would get jealous. I felt exhausted, tired of so much pretending.

'I'm sorry,' I whispered.

'Fix it!' Colin shouted, making me jump.

'I will.'

'Just DO IT!'

And with that he was gone. I sat upstairs for a bit and then turned on my TV. I didn't feel like going back downstairs and facing my sister and my mum. Sometimes it seemed like I could never do the right thing. I tried hard to fulfil my duties to the Church, to make Colin happy, to please the Gods and get through my studies. But it was so hard.

I curled up under my duvet and shut my eyes. I couldn't for the life of me work out why Colin was so determined to create this relationship between Thomas and me. Looking back now, I see there was something else at work and it had to do with my mum. After all, the fake relationship had started soon after my mum got pregnant. Colin was much cleverer than I realized. He was covering his tracks.

'That was Sandra.' Elaine turned to me after putting down her mobile phone. 'Your mum has had the baby: a little boy. They're both doing fine.'

I smiled, genuinely happy for the first time in ages. It was 5 October, a few days after my fifteenth birthday, and I was in Tenby for the weekend with Elaine and Hope. An invite to join them in the caravan was actually a rare occurrence but I guessed Colin had made them take me that weekend because my mum had gone into labour. We'd spent a wet and windy two days playing games of Uno and watching Disney videos on the tiny portable TV mounted on the wall. Frankly it was nice to have a change of scenery, and to be away from Colin and Thomas for a few days, away from Colin's constant demands and watchful eyes. Hope had been really kind to me, too, so it made me feel like maybe she didn't hate me after all. But then, after the call, I caught her and Elaine exchange a look, just the tiniest flicker of the eyes towards one another. I tried to ignore it.

'What should we do?' I asked then. I didn't want to be stuck in Tenby while my new brother was at home.

'She won't be in the hospital long,' Elaine said, and started bustling about, putting cups into the sink and clearing up our plates from lunch. 'I expect she'll be home by tonight. We'll get you back there so you can see your baby brother.'

All the way back that evening, I was so excited I could hardly sit still. Horizontal rain lashed the windows, as strong gusts rocked the car from side to side, but I hardly noticed. I just wanted to see the baby – my brother!

It was teatime and already dark by the time we pulled into our driveway. I jumped out and ran straight into the house. Mum sat in the living room, holding a tiny bundle of blue blankets with a fuzzy tuft of raven-black hair sticking out the top. For the first time in years she looked at me and smiled.

'Come and see,' she beamed. 'He's beautiful.'

I moved slowly towards her, not wanting to break the spell. My mum seemed to be radiating love and warmth at this moment; her face looked softer and her eyes shone. I went to sit next to her on the sofa and peeked into her arms, pulling aside the blanket to get a good look at my brother. He was gorgeous! A round, creased face with gently closed eyelids and chubby little hands curled at his cheeks.

'Ah, he's so tiny!' I exclaimed. 'He's beautiful, Mum, really beautiful.'

She looked up at me and smiled again – it was so natural and genuine, but it was the first time in years I'd seen her look like this and I felt like crying. The next second she turned back to the baby, rearranging the blankets around his face.

'I'm calling him Ahmose. It means "Son of the God" in Egyptian – we'll just call him Moses. OK?'

I nodded, so happy. I had a lovely baby brother and my mother seemed to have changed overnight.

For the next few weeks I took every opportunity to hold and play with Moses – he was adorable and I couldn't keep my hands off him. Mum lavished tons of love on him too. It was as if her jagged edges smoothed out when she was around him. Her eyes flashed less, her voice became quieter – it was a subtle change but it felt like our whole household was happier thanks to Moses. His presence soothed us all. Yet I couldn't help feeling the sharp pain of rejection the first time I realized that it was him she loved, not me.

One day I saw her crooning into his cot and the next moment she looked at me, it was as if someone had switched out the lights. Her eyes turned dull and face went blank – she looked straight through me and in that minute I knew it was all for him. I was jealous of him. I couldn't help it. I still longed for my mother's love, and to see it so liberally sprinkled over this tiny boy and withheld from me entirely was agonizing.

As for the rest of the Church, the baby's name made things even harder. Everyone knew Ahmose was the Egyptian name for Son of God, and they knew what this meant – that he was Colin's son. And although nobody said it out loud, there was more hostility to us than ever before. I was certainly never invited to Tenby again.

Chapter 9

Pete

'So, Annabelle, what did you get up to at the weekend?'

The question came from Kelly, one of the girls who worked with me at Julie's Beauty. It was a reasonable question. After all, most people do things at the weekend – they visit pubs and clubs or they go to the cinema or out for a meal. That is what normal people do. Not me though, I didn't live a normal life. At sixteen I had still never been to a cinema or seen the inside of a pub or club. I'd never been taken to a restaurant or gone inside a shop on my own. My life was still confined to home and the Church, so it was hard to know how to answer Kelly.

In the past year I'd knuckled down to my GCSEs and managed to pass five, which was amazing considering how far behind I'd been at fourteen. I was pleased and wanted to go to catering college. I liked the idea of learning how to cook – at home my mum didn't make much of an effort and we never had any ingredients in the house to make really good meals from scratch. The one thing she cooked really well, though, was roast potatoes, and she used to do these with frozen pies and frozen vegetables.

They were lovely but they were the high point of her culinary efforts. Most of the time, it was meals straight from the freezer – burgers, sausages, fish fingers or chips. Occasionally we were treated to some beans or scrambled eggs, but that was it. There was never any fresh meat or fish in our house. I never once saw an onion in our kitchen, a raw mushroom or a bulb of garlic.

I could boil pasta and make toast – that was about it. I didn't even really know how to cook an egg properly. I'd seen these things on TV of course, and loved watching celebrity cooks like Jamie Oliver and Gordon Ramsay. Watching Jamie slam pans of delicious stuff in his oven, squeeze lemons, grate cheese and chop endless vegetables, I was intrigued. There was so much more to know about food.

Unfortunately Colin said no to catering college because it was too far from our house. But I still wanted to learn a trade, so I applied to do a beauty therapy course at my local college and was thrilled when I was accepted. Colin was pleased too – after all, the longer I was in education, the longer my mum would get benefits for me.

Now I did two days a week at college and one day at Julie's Beauty Salon, where I worked as a junior intern, learning how to do the hands-on jobs like waxing, massage, manicures and pedicures. I loved it. For the first time I was learning how to do proper girlie stuff – I could spend all day chatting about hair and make-up and nobody minded because now it was my job! The first time I got my eyebrows waxed was fantastic. There was me and the other intern, Kelly, and though we weren't paid we were allowed to keep our tips and I used this money to get my lunches during the week.

Julie had a number of other beauty therapists and hairdressers who worked in her shop and I was so happy to be around other girls my age. Once a week, every Tuesday, I felt like a normal young girl. The only problem was the small talk – I had to do an awful lot of lying to cover up the fact that my life was so very different.

After all, it was pretty unusual that a girl my age had never chosen her own clothes from a shop or tasted alcohol. While everyone else was going out at the weekends, I was staying in, looking after my baby brother because Mum was now working weekends for the Church. In fact, I was so used to staying in at this point that it didn't even occur to me to want to go out. I had spent so long at home that the outside world scared me. Being among people made me feel horribly anxious and, on the rare occasions I was allowed to accompany my mum on her shopping trips to Asda, I spent the whole time frightened and praying for it to be over. I much preferred being at home with Moses.

By now the meetings and ceremonies had more or less stopped completely. I certainly hadn't dressed in my ceremonial robes for a good year or so. Colin didn't seem interested in running meetings for the Church any more, which was a great relief. I'd always found them long, incomprehensible and boring as hell, with each hour dragging by in a fug of strange words and phrases which didn't make sense to my young ears. Of course, my life was still dominated by the Church, and now Colin had Mum and a few others working for the Church directly.

Mum's work for the Church was a mystery to me and I knew better than to ask. All I knew was that she left on Friday afternoon and was back at lunchtime on Monday, by which time she'd be really tired and head straight to bed. For the rest of the week she was useless, lying around in bed or on the sofa. She stopped paying attention to Moses. When he cried, she couldn't be bothered to go to him, so it usually ended up being me who comforted him at night, changed his nappies or fed him his bottles. I didn't mind. I adored my baby brother and, as long as I could do my beauty therapy course and work at Julie's, then I was happy to spend the rest of my time at home with him.

Still, it was a strain to keep up with the small talk. A tiny, middle-aged lady with enormous bouffant hair and wrists weighed down with gold bangles, Julie liked to natter and encouraged us to chat to the clients. It helped, she told us, to establish a relationship and put them at their ease. I listened carefully to her advice because I wanted to do well. As for the other girls who worked in the salon, I tried my best to fit in.

'I went out in Tenby this weekend,' I told Kelly, as casually as I could. 'I don't usually go out in Kidwelly.'

This was a safe response – the girls around there didn't spend much time in Tenby, so they couldn't ask me about specific clubs or pubs. This seemed to satisfy Kelly and she started rambling on about her weekend getting pissed with her friends, and how she went to a club on Saturday night and ended up meeting some lad whom she snogged and now she was waiting for him to call.

I smiled as she described the boy she liked – I'd never known what it meant to 'like' someone in this way but I was excited for her. I tried to focus on Kelly, putting out of my mind what Colin had told me the night before, that there was another test on the way and he was planning to send someone round to see me.

'Give him oral sex and then normal sex. Right?'

I'd nodded. Oral and then normal.

'Stop that!' Mum yelled at me from the hallway. 'I can see what you're doing. Stop it!'

I quickly pulled my hands away from the tumble dryer. They were frozen numb and the tumble dryer was so warm it was hard to resist. It was still early October but for some reason it was freezing. I'd run back from the bus stop after my day at Julie's and nearly slipped on a patch of ice that had formed on the pavement. My breath escaped my mouth in a visible plume, as I wobbled then righted myself. My nose stung from the cold and I rubbed the tip with my bare fingers. I didn't even have any gloves. Oh, God, it was cold!

I fell in the front door that evening and was delighted to hear the deep rumble of the tumble dryer spinning round. After stomping out my frozen toes on the mat, I headed straight for the kitchen and placed my white fingers on the top of the dryer. Ohhhh! That was lovely!

'Stop it!' Mum shouted again. 'I've told you before – you'll get chilblains. Just let them warm up naturally.'

Mum walked in, scowling, and dipped her head down to look inside the oven.

'Your tea's ready,' she said. 'Chicken burger, beans and chips. Go on, get to the table now. You've got to eat quickly tonight.'

'Why?'

'You've got someone coming round to see you, that's why.' This must be the next test.

'Who is it?' I wanted to know.

'It's Pete – now go on, get to the table.'

Pete? Pete was coming to see me? I walked slowly to the kitchen table and lowered myself into the seat. *Pete?* Pete was Griff's son. He was the same age as me – well, physically anyway. Pete actually had learning disabilities, which meant he had the mental age of a child. He often had no idea what was really going on. Though I enjoyed playing with him when I was a little girl, it felt like I'd left him far behind, stuck in perpetual childhood. When I thought of Pete I didn't think of him as a teenager, as someone my own age, he was more like a ten-year-old boy. Mum threw the full plate in front of me but at that moment my appetite fled. Next to me, Olivia tucked into her food and Mum spoon-fed Moses a jar of pureed bolognese in his high chair, occasionally dabbing at his chin with the bottom corner of his cloth bib.

Twenty minutes later my burger and chips were still there, getting colder by the minute.

'What's wrong with you?' Mum asked, as she nodded towards my uneaten tea.

'I'm not that hungry,' I told her. My stomach was in knots and I couldn't get anything down. *How could Colin make me have sex with Pete?* It didn't seem right. Until this moment all the people I'd been made to have sex with had been older than me, more experienced. They had taken the lead and I had just followed and done what I was told. This was different. Did Pete even know what sex was? He was a child.

The chime of the doorbell made me jump but Mum instructed me to stay in the kitchen with my siblings while she showed Pete into the living room.

Then she came back into the kitchen and, without looking in my direction, she went straight to her 'special drawer', the one over the bin which none of us were allowed to go in. She beckoned me over and put a condom into my hand, out of sight of Olivia, who had polished off her own tea and was now hoovering up my plate of chips. I didn't know if she was deliberately keeping her eyes down to avoid seeing something or whether she really was fixated with the food. Either way, I appreciated her lack of curiosity.

'You've got to put this on him with your mouth,' Mum whispered.

'What does he know?' I whispered back, taking the small packet and placing it in my jeans pocket. I needed reassurance. I needed to know the extent to which I had to take charge of this situation.

'Just get in there,' Mum hissed. 'It'll be fine.'

I didn't feel fine at this point. My stomach was like a pit of writhing snakes as I crossed the corridor and walked reluctantly into the living room to find Pete sitting taut and upright on the edge of the sofa. His hands were laced together in his lap, his knees jiggled nervously up and down and he turned and smiled stupidly at me when I walked in.

'Hello Annabelle!' he shouted, too loudly.

'Hi Pete,' I mumbled back.

Mum came in after me, holding what looked like a small video camera. She looked up at me briefly and my face must have registered the shock. *What was she even doing in here? Was she going to watch? And what was that in her hand?*

'Colin's asked me to record it,' she explained, fiddling with the buttons on the side of the machine.

Oh great! This was getting better and better by the minute. I shook my head now – this was all too much. I wanted to get it over and done with. As for Pete, he was looking everywhere round the room, except at me. His hand went to the back of his neck and he rubbed his head absent-mindedly. His fine, strawberry-blonde hair flopped over blue eyes, flecked with anxiety, and he chewed on his bottom lip. He knew what was happening, I could tell, but he seemed lost and uncomfortable.

I knelt down in front of him and undid the buttons on his stonewashed jeans – then, in one movement, I pulled the jeans and his boxer shorts down around his ankles. He giggled nervously, like a little boy.

Keep it together, Pete. Just try and keep it together.

This was painful but I knew neither of us had any choice in the matter – we had to get through it. I took his penis in my hand and then lowered my mouth towards him. When he started to get hard I pulled the condom out of my pocket, ripped open the packet and slid it on with my mouth, as my mum had instructed me.

By now moaning noises were escaping from Pete, in between inappropriate little laughs. He wasn't going to be able to do this on his own, I knew that, so I took off my jeans and lay down on the floor, pulling him on top of me. I was leading it. For the first time, I was in control of the situation and I hated every minute. In my heart, I knew this was wrong. I took him in my hand and gently guided him inside me. Up close he smelt clean and freshly-scrubbed – innocent. I swallowed hard – God, this was awful. Gradually he started to move and I closed my eyes, trying to do that thing where my mind goes somewhere else. I wanted to be on the beach again – or in the woods or the fields. Anywhere but here! But I couldn't disappear because I kept getting distracted by my mum, who was now circling me and Pete as we lay on the floor, her eye stuck to the viewer of the camcorder, recording it all.

She was trying to get us from every angle and, each time she did a circuit and came close to my head, I turned to face the other way so she couldn't film my face. All I wanted to do was get it over with but she was at my shoulder every thirty seconds, shoving a camera in my face. On her third lap she mimed at me: 'Enjoy yourself. MOVE!'

Just then I felt Pete pull out of me and sit back on his knees, scratching his neck again and snickering. His looked pained and then my heart went out to him. What in the world was he thinking?

'I . . . uh . . . I can't do it with you . . . erm . . . recording,' he stuttered at my mum. She stared at him as he pulled his jeans up. He got to his feet and, for a few seconds, hopped uncertainly from one foot to the other, rubbing his head up and down, clearly at a loss. He was so distressed I wanted to go to him then and put my arms around him. I wanted to let him know that it was OK, that he didn't have to do anything. I felt wretched with the whole situation and was relieved when he left the room and walked out the front door.

I sat up then and pulled my trousers back up. I looked over at my mum – she flicked off the video camera and wandered away without saying a word. I stayed on the floor for a bit, bewildered and upset. The whole thing had felt wrong, and at this point I didn't really know why. Was I upset because I'd failed the test? Or was there something else? I knew I hadn't wanted to have sex with Pete but at this stage I didn't know why it made me feel so terrible.

I looked at the clock on the wall – it was still only 6.30 p.m. A little while later Olivia and Moses came back in the living room and someone switched on the TV for *EastEnders*. I tried to put the memory of what I'd done with Pete to the back of my mind, and it was only later, alone in my bed, that the guilty feelings surfaced. For the first time I had been the one in control and it was Pete who'd had the worst thing happen to him. How far would this go? I wondered in the darkness. How many others would there be?

Chapter 10

Despair

I stared down at the pile of white pills in the palm of my left hand and with the forefinger of my right hand I moved them around. One, two, three, four, five, six . . . I counted out twenty-four in total. Twenty-four paracetamol. Was it enough? I didn't know. I hoped so. I looked out the window on another cold January night, sheets of rain with dark clouds swirling over our heads. Right then, I wanted so much to just go to sleep and never wake up again.

On my TV, the video *Mary Poppins* was playing for the millionth time – Mary sang 'A Spoonful of Sugar'. I moved the pills around in my hand again. I just hoped the tablets were enough to kill myself.

It's funny. Until that moment, I'd never thought about dying before. But now it felt like the answer to all my problems – in one night I could wipe out all the despair, the pain, the anxiety and the horror. It felt like my life was just one unending list of horrible, horrible events. It had been over two months since that encounter with Pete and, although Colin had never mentioned it to me, I couldn't get it out of my mind. I felt so rotten about what we had done. Thankfully it had never happened again but I was still made to have sex regularly with Colin, Thomas and sometimes Colin and my mum.

I didn't know who I was going to have sex with from one night to the next. Colin was more demanding than ever before. I wasn't trying hard enough to please him, he said. The Gods were displeased. I didn't show enough jealousy. I had to want him completely in order to become his Scarlet Woman. In the next breath, he was ordering me to sleep with Thomas. Then he'd turn me over and have sex with me from behind, roughly. These days he liked being rough with me; he liked to give me pain. Still, it barely registered what he did to me physically. I had no feelings about my own body any more – it didn't even belong to me, really. Day after day, night after night, it was all the same thing. Nothing gave me pleasure any more – I was going through the motions of my life like a machine, without any connection to myself let alone anyone else. Little wonder I was tired of it all and wanted to go to sleep.

It didn't occur to me that at seventeen years old I could leave home. It just didn't present itself to me as an option because leaving home was scarier than death. Colin had told me a number of times that if I ever tried to leave the Church would turn its back on me and I would be completely alone. I would have nothing and nobody. This was truly terrifying. I had been kept apart from the big wide world and as a consequence I was frightened of it.

I'd never been allowed to explore the park at the end of my

road, let alone a shopping mall or Kidwelly town centre. It was all so removed from most people's experience of their normal environment that the local park might as well have been the moon! If I left the Church and fell out of favour with the Gods then I would no longer be protected. I could get hit by a car or stabbed in the street or attacked by a stranger. Without their protection I would live my life in constant fear of the worst happening. To me, that felt worse than death.

It's not like we had any computers or smartphones at home to allow me to connect to people outside – unlike the rest of my peers, I was a stranger to technology. I'd never been on Facebook or seen a social network site. I was seventeen on the outside but, when it came to making my own choices or learning about the world, I was a child.

Colin had kept me completely dependent on the Church and I couldn't imagine my life without it. It was all I'd ever known. If I left, how would I earn money? Where would I live? Who would help me? These questions had no answers in my mind. No, losing the Church was inconceivable.

But the fact was I couldn't cope any more. I felt worthless. I didn't want to be having sex with anyone, especially my own mother. It was shortly after Moses was born that I started to get an inkling that pills could be dangerous. Before then, I didn't really know. We weren't allowed to go to the doctor, so I hadn't had much contact with medicines. The only thing I'd seen were packets of paracetamol, which Mum took for her period pains. She told me to put the pills away in the bathroom cupboard because they could hurt the baby. Over the next few months I found out more – taking too many could be fatal. I wasn't scared. All I was frightened of was more of the same. If I died then at least Colin had to leave me in peace.

Mum kept the packet of paracetamol in the bathroom cupboard and, that night, just after dinner, I'd gone upstairs and taken it. It was a small white cardboard box containing two silver foil packets. I'd stashed the box under my jumper, as I tiptoed from the bathroom to my bedroom and then quietly shut the door behind me.

My sister and I shared a bunk bed these days, and now I clambered onto my mattress on the bottom. Turning my back to the door, I popped the pills through the foil one by one, watching as they tumbled gently into my lap. Mum was downstairs with Olivia and Moses, watching TV as usual. If anyone came upstairs I'd hear their footsteps and it would be easy enough to hide the pills with the corner of the duvet.

I sighed. Twenty-four was a lot for someone who found it difficult to swallow pills. I let them all fall into my lap again and then took one pill and, placing my thumbnails against the small indentation in the centre, pushed hard, breaking it in half. I placed the two halves in a new pile in front of my crossed legs. Then I did the same with another, and another, and another. Tiny spots of white powder landed on my black trousers as each pill cracked. The new pile, though larger, seemed much more manageable.

On the TV, Julie Andrews and Dick Van Dyke crooned arm-in-arm and I began to swallow the halves one by one, following each with a sip of water from the glass next to my bed. I went slowly, taking a few breaths between each pill. My eyes were drawn up towards the TV – it was the scene where they all jumped into Bert's chalk drawing on the pavement. In a magical puff of rainbow-coloured smoke, Mary's dowdy governess clothes were replaced by a gorgeous lacy white dress and bright red sash corset. Bert, no longer a grime-ridden chimney sweep, now wore a smart candy-striped blazer. He began to sing – his chipper cockney melody describing the beautiful morning, the blue sky, daffodils and green grass made all the lovelier by having Mary at his side. He was so happy he felt like he could fly away.

Meanwhile, my pile of pills was gradually decreasing. How many had I taken now – ten, twelve maybe? I wondered how long it would take for the drugs to start working. Would I get through them before I started to feel tired? The sound from the TV was bright and familiar – cartoon birds flitted about the imaginary woodland scene as Bert sung. Now he was in the farmyard and the horse was joining him in the verse.

I loved this scene, this song, this film. Normally I would sing along, hugging my monkey toy tight. But right this minute I didn't want to sing. I didn't even want to hear out the rest of the song. I just wanted to go to sleep. I flicked off the TV and gathered the rest of the pill halves in my hand. Quickly, I gulped down one after another with a sharp little sip between each. I wanted death to come quickly. I wanted nothing but oblivion. Blissful, peaceful, final death. Now that I had started this, I needed to get it over with quickly, so I gulped the last of the pill halves back with the rest of the water, put the glass under my bed and changed into my pyjamas. Then I turned off the light and climbed under my duvet.

I closed my eyes, eager to meet death in the painless cradle of sleep, but still my mind raced, excited by the thought of the transformation ahead. What would it feel like? How long would it take? Would it hurt? I checked myself for strange feelings, listening to my heart drumming in my chest, inhaling and exhaling loudly to try and hear if my breathing was shaky. I treated my death like a fascinating science experiment, shut off as I was from my feelings.

With my left hand, I felt along my right arm for signs that my body was changing temperature. I didn't know what I was looking for exactly but I made a thorough inventory of myself just to see if I could track the change from life to death. Somewhat disappointingly, I didn't feel any different from normal. And this made me panic, holding back the possibility of sleep. What if I hadn't taken enough?

I don't know how long I'd been in bed before I heard the familiar turn of the door handle and the room was flooded with light. I squinted against the brightness. Mum stood in the doorframe, her long dark hair swishing softly down her back. She stood like that for ages, holding onto the doorknob, not speaking. She didn't come in. *Go away*, I said to her in my head. *JUST GO AWAY!* But I didn't say anything out loud – I lay still, hoping she would think I was asleep.

After a while I became exasperated.

'What? What is it?' I spoke into the darkness. I just wanted to be left alone to get on with dying. I didn't want her interfering.

'What are you doing?' she asked.

'I'm going to sleep. Well, trying, at least,' I replied testily. I mean, wasn't that obvious?

'Why are you going to bed so early?'

'I'm tired.'

And that was it. The door clicked shut as she left. That was my last conversation with my mother, I told myself, as I felt a strange dragging feeling on the corners of my mind, like the whumping motion of an engine slowly coming to a stop. The last thing my mother said to me was: 'Why are you going to bed so early?' I didn't feel sad. It was a curious thing, that was all.

I let my mind float over the top of this idea for a while, observing my reaction to my mother's final goodbye, turning it over and around to look at it from different sides. Why are you going to bed so early? So early. Early. Good night. Good night. Good night. Now I watched myself as if from far away. I was a girl in a film, a girl jumping into an imaginary scene, like a chalk drawing, and being transported far away, to a place where the sun shone, where cartoon rabbits jumped at your feet and people sung to each other and wore pretty dresses and the sky was blue . . .

Owch! I felt a sharp pain across the back of my head.

What was that?

Then a voice: 'Get up!'

My sister's voice, still thick with sleep, punctured my deep slumber. She lolloped off in the direction of the bathroom. Urgh . . . my head, my stomach. I could hardly move. It felt like I'd gone ten rounds with Mike Tyson. For a while I just lay there, waves of nausea sliding up my throat. Why did I feel so awful? My head was clogged with confusion and my throat, dry and scratchy.

The pills! In a flash the whole thing came back to me. My eyes shot open. It hadn't worked. I was alive. Why hadn't it worked? Now the sickness was joined by disappointment and depression. As well as everything else, I felt sick as a dog. My sister walked back past me from the bathroom and shoved at my shoulder, making me rock. The bile rose again.

'I said get up!'

I hated it when she did this and I always told her to just leave me, but she liked to wind me up. I don't know why. In truth, I didn't have much to do with Olivia. She annoyed me so I tried to stay out of her way. She was twelve now, about the same age I was when Colin started having sex with me, but I didn't worry. He didn't seem interested and never called for her when he was round our house.

'What's wrong with you this morning?' she asked, as she pulled off her pyjamas, chucked them in a corner and clambered into her school uniform. I watched her from my bed, feeling too ill to move.

'Nothing. I just don't feel very well, that's all.'

Now she sat on the floor to pull on her socks and shoes. She glanced briefly at the clock on our wardrobe. 'Yeah, well, you're going to be late if you don't get up soon. It's eight o'clock.'

'OK, OK. Just give me a minute.'

I dipped my head under the bed and saw the glass of water and the empty Paracetamol packets. What was I going to do

with the packets? I hadn't thought this far ahead. I didn't plan
to be alive this morning. If I threw them in the bin, Mum would
find them and then she'd know what I'd done. There had been
a full box of twenty-four yesterday. Quietly I reached under the
bed and retrieved the two foil pill packets and slid them both
back into the cardboard box. Then, after hauling myself out of
bed, I went back to the bathroom and returned the box to the
bathroom cupboard. As soon as I had enough money saved up
from my tips I would buy a new box of paracetamol. That way
nobody would know what I'd done.

I dressed that morning, still groggy, and went to college as
usual. It was a fairly normal day and, apart from feeling nau-
seous, I didn't seem to bear any lasting damage from taking the
pills the night before. Hope was studying at the same college as
me and at lunchtime she asked if I wanted to go round to her
house that night to do her nails. Of course, I jumped at the
chance – Hope rarely spoke to me these days so it was lovely to
be invited over and I relished every opportunity to practise my
manicures. That night I didn't waste any time. I went straight
home and changed out of my college uniform – a white tunic
over black trousers – before picking up my special beauty case
that had all my manicure stuff in it. I wheeled the large black
case straight round to Hope's.

'Here, let's do it in my room,' she said. I wasn't there five
minutes before Colin put his head round Hope's bedroom door.
I was about to start working on her cuticles.

'You,' he pointed at me. 'I want a word with you.'

Sighing, I put down Hope's hand and told her to soak both

of them in the bowl of warm water. Then I followed him down the stairs into the living room.

'Is there anything you want to tell me?' he asked.

'No,' I replied, my face a mask.

'We know that you took the tablets.'

Suddenly my heart jumped. How did he know? I was frightened. What would I tell him? I expected him to ask me next why I had tried to kill myself. But, strangely, he didn't.

Instead he said: 'It's not going to work because you're protected by the Gods. The Gods will always protect you, even from yourself and your stupid mistakes.'

What?

I was so confused. Is this why it hadn't worked? Were the Gods really protecting me? If Colin wasn't speaking to the Gods, then how did he know what I'd done last night? I didn't know what to say. I stood there, looking at him, unable to speak a word.

I didn't try to take my life again – I knew now there was no point. It was never going to be over; the Gods were always watching and they would stop it from working. Colin was always going to be there, in life and death. There was no escape.

Chapter 11

A Change

The bell above the shop door jangled as I fell into Julie's Beauty Salon, flustered and upset.

'I'm so sorry, Julie,' I said, wheeling my beauty case behind me. I'd missed my last two placements at the salon so today, 12 June, I was determined to get to work. But having spent the first half of the morning with my head down the toilet bowl, desperately trying to stop dry heaving, I was horribly late.

'Don't worry, Petal. Just get yourself changed and sort yourself out,' Julie called, barely looking up from buffing a customer's nails. The chemical smell of nail polish remover filled my nostrils and, once again, I felt my stomach lurch. I moved quickly to the back room, where I changed into my white tunic, but as I came back into the salon another wave of nausea hit me and I had to make a quick grab for the counter.

'Whatever's the matter, Annabelle?' Julie looked up now and her face fell in dismay. 'Oh, my lovely, you don't look well at all. Look 'ere, you're pale as anything.'

She put her palm to my forehead, her eyes creased with concern, and I thought at that moment I might cry.

'I'm OK,' I told her, though I still clung to the counter, knowing that any sudden movement may result in me retching all over her salon. I breathed in and out, my eyes closed. Finally I felt well enough to speak.

'I've just had this . . . erm . . . this infection. And that's why I haven't been in for the last two weeks. I'm really sorry, Julie.'

Julie gestured for one of the other girls to take over the manicure and she came over to see me. Gently, she took my arm and led me into the back room.

'Why don't you tell me all about it?' she smiled, easing me into a foldaway chair next to a small metal table in the centre of the room. As she filled the kettle, I looked about me – in contrast to the front of the shop, which was nicely decorated with pine floors and white walls, here pale-green paint peeled off the walls and the floor was patterned with old-fashioned black and white lino. The small room was lit by a bare bulb hanging from the ceiling.

'Oh, it's nothing really. My periods have been all funny for the last few weeks,' I told her. 'I'm pretty sure it's just an infection *down there* because I've been feeling sick a lot. I've been on these antibiotics for the last three days and I thought they were working but this morning I threw up again.'

I sighed and looked down at my hands in my lap. I had really hoped that the pills Colin had given me would clear up the infection. As usual, I wasn't allowed to see a doctor – instead Colin had given me a course of antibiotics from his own medicine cabinet. But after six doses I felt no better.

'Oh, my love, that sounds awful,' Julie said, and put her hand on mine. Then she narrowed her eyes and asked me very slowly: 'But are you sure it's an infection, Annabelle?'

I tipped my head to one side, confused. What did she mean? At that moment Michelle, one of the other beauty therapists, wandered in.

'All right, Annabelle?' she asked. 'You been ill or sommat?'

'I think she could be pregnant,' said Julie, looking directly at me.

'What?' I exploded. 'I'm not pregnant. There's no way!'

'Really?' Julie replied. 'You've done a pregnancy test then?'

'Well, no, I haven't, but I know I can't be pregnant.'

'How do you know if you haven't done a test? I mean, from what you're telling me, it does sound awfully like the early signs of pregnancy. I should know, love. I've had four myself!'

She smiled at me then, trying to make me feel better. It's true I hadn't done a test, but how could I tell her that I couldn't be pregnant because I was protected by the Gods? Colin had stopped using condoms with me years before, though I always used one with Thomas. When I'd asked Colin about the possibility of falling pregnant he'd told me not to worry. He'd laughed – nothing was going to happen unless he wanted it. The Gods were protecting me at all times.

In the silence, Julie spoke again: 'Look, why don't you get yourself down the chemist and pick up a pregnancy test? It wouldn't do any harm just to check. Then you'll know for sure. After all, you don't want to be taking antibiotics if you've got a baby in there.'

'I can't be pregnant,' I repeated quietly. 'I just can't.'

'Hmmm . . . well, let's see. What do you think? Look, here's some change.'

She fished a few coins out of her tunic pocket then turned back to Michelle: 'Go with her to the pharmacy down the road. They do them cheap ones. Go on.'

So Michelle took me to the pharmacy at the end of the shopping arcade and we came away with the cheapest pregnancy test they sold – a small pot with a stick for £2.50. Michelle chatted all the way there and back – she had a new bloke and he'd taken her out last night but she wasn't sure she liked him. He was into cars and he ate with his fingers. She didn't like that. I nodded but I was only half-listening, resentful about being dragged into this pantomime – it was all a nonsense! I was only going along to placate Julie. I knew I couldn't be pregnant.

Once we got back, Julie, now working on another client, sent me into the little toilet across the hallway to fill up the pot with wee and, when I returned to the back room, Michelle dipped in the stick. Straight away, two red lines appeared on the stick.

'Oh my God!' Michelle exclaimed.

'What? What does that mean?'

'Two lines! It means you're pregnant. Look! Both lines are really clear and strong.'

I couldn't believe it. I *still* couldn't believe it. I stared at the stick for a little while then I asked Michelle in a small, hopeful voice: 'Is the test ever wrong?'

She picked up the box and started reading.

'It says here 99.9 per cent right every time,' she tapped the box assuredly with her sparkly pink nails. 'I don't think it would say you were pregnant if you weren't.'

I nodded then turned down the hallway.

'She's probably going to be sick again,' I heard Michelle whispering to Julie, who had now reappeared in the back room. 'You were right, she *is* pregnant. Both lines came up instantly – whoosh! Just like that – no messing around.'

But I didn't need to throw up. For the first time in years I felt a stinging sensation behind my eyes and I knew at any second the tears would start to fall. I rushed into the toilet, slammed the door shut, then sat with my head in my hands and let the unfamiliar feelings overtake me. First I started to shake, uncontrollably from the pit of my stomach right up my ribcage and to my shoulders. On and on it went, this silent shaking, and then a sob and suddenly a strangled wail escaped me. My hands flew to my mouth as I tried to smother the sound, but I couldn't. Now the tears fell and I gave myself over to it completely. I sat and bawled my eyes out.

A baby? A child? I couldn't have a child – I was still a child myself! I'd done nothing in my life. Nothing! If I had a baby I would never achieve anything. And what sort of life would the baby have? I couldn't bring another life into my world – it wasn't right. Then it hit me, I had to tell Colin. Yes, I would tell Colin and he would make it all right again. Colin had the power to change this!

The rest of the day passed by in a blur. Julie asked me if I was all right and I told her I was fine, just a little shocked.

'How do you feel about the situation?' she asked kindly.

'I don't know. I wasn't expecting it.'

'No, of course not. Well, don't worry. There's lots of time to think about things.'

I tried to put the baby out of my mind while I got on with my appointments that day, but it kept popping into my head at the strangest times. I couldn't imagine a life growing inside me – the idea of it was terrifying. I couldn't wait for the day to be over so I could go home and tell Colin. He'd know what to do. He was everything to me: my father, lover, protector and leader. I knew that Colin could put this right again.

It was still warm outside when I got home at 6 p.m. that evening. Mum was sat talking to Colin at our kitchen table.

I lingered in the doorway: 'Erm, Colin, can I have a word with you, please?'

He looked at me briefly then his eyes flicked back to Mum and he nodded, a signal for her to leave. She got up and brushed past my shoulder as she walked out. I took her place at the kitchen table.

'I need to tell you something,' I began, my heart in my mouth. 'I'm pregnant.'

For a split second, I saw shock.

Colin's eyes widened, his mouth fell open and he was silent. I waited. A couple of seconds passed before he composed his face and looked down, taking a draw from his cigarette.

'We already knew that,' he exhaled.

I don't believe you.

For the first time in my life I knew that he was lying and it surprised me. I saw his reaction! You can't fake shock. He was genuinely surprised when I told him I was pregnant, so I didn't buy it when he said he, or rather, he and the Gods, already knew that. He didn't. They didn't! It was unnerving to realize that Colin hadn't known I was pregnant; he said all along that I was protected, unless he wanted me to get pregnant. If I had got pregnant without him wanting it, how had this happened?

He leaned in now and spoke quickly and quietly: 'We want you to get rid of it.'

Relief now flooded my body. *Thank God!* It's all I wanted to hear.

'I want to get rid of it as well,' I told him.

'Right, well, I'll give you a bit of time to think about things then I'll come in and see you tonight. In the meantime I think you better tell your mum.'

'What? Why?'

'I think she'd better know the truth.'

'I don't want to . . .'

'JACKIE!' It was too late, he was already yelling for her. She rolled in, her usual cold, slow swagger, one hand on her hip.

'What?'

'Jackie, Annabelle here has got something to tell you.'

I didn't want to do this. Despite everything that had happened, everything she had done to me, I didn't want to let her down. She was still my mum and I didn't want to disappoint her.

'I'm pregnant,' I said quietly.

'Yeah, I knew that. I could tell.'

There was no shock on Mum's part – just her usual blankness. I don't know how she could tell. I was still as thin as a rake.

'You want to try keeping your legs crossed a bit more,' she drawled, barely breaking step as she walked out into the garden. That was it. I felt myself crumble. How could she be so callous? At that moment, I needed love and reassurance. I needed a mother. Of course it was more than I could ever expect from her. Colin smirked at me: 'I'll be round later. Be ready.'

So that night, after a long and exhausting day, I waited up for Colin until he came in the back door at midnight. When he walked into the living room I pulled my dressing gown tight around me. I was cold now and so tired.

'The baby's yours, you know,' I told him when he appeared.

He smiled and shook his head as he sat on the sofa next to me: 'No, no. No, it isn't.'

'It is,' I assured him. 'I use a condom with Thomas. It can't be his. Anyway, I want to get rid of it.'

'Well, that is your will, Annabelle,' he replied, taking hold of the rope cord of my dressing gown. 'Now get undressed and lie down.'

The next day I was at home with Moses since Mum had to work. I still didn't know where she went or what she did for half the week. All I knew was that on Thursday afternoons Shelly picked her up in her car and we didn't see either of them again until Monday. It used to be Fridays, but as time went on she started leaving on Thursdays. Sometimes Millie went with them, but not every time.

By now Moses was eighteen months old and he spent so much time with me he thought I was his mum. I didn't mind – Moses was the one nice thing in my life. To him, I was the most important person in the world and he'd follow me from room to room when we were together in the house. I'm sure it irritated my mum when she heard him babbling 'Mama Mama' at me, but then what did she expect? She left him in my care most of the time so she couldn't complain when he mistook me for his mother.

I loved playing with Moses and I lived for his smile. Seeing his little face light up and hearing his delighted squeals when I chased him down the hallway made my day. He was a lovely little boy and when I was with him I found myself smiling or laughing for real. Our house had really filled up in the past year; we now had Colin's eldest son Damian living with us too. Damian had been in a bit of trouble when he was younger so he'd been sent to England to live with relatives for a few years. Now he was back in the Church, but Colin didn't like his sons living under his roof so Damian had our box room.

For the most part, he was easy and undemanding. He got up early each morning for his job at the local supermarket and, when he was home, he spent most of his time in his bedroom, which was an absolute pit. I tried not to go in there because it was his space but whenever he left the door open I caught sight of the mess inside – there were old, mouldy plates of food, dirty boxer shorts and abandoned cups of tea. Urgh! It was disgusting.

Now that Mum was away most of the time, it was up to me to run the house, look after the kids, do all the cooking and the cleaning and washing and sorting out the cats. Sakkara now had a mate – another Siamese cat that Colin had brought in – and he wouldn't leave her alone. She'd already had three litters, which Colin had sold off, and now she was pregnant again. I felt sorry for the poor thing – she barely got rid of one litter before she was up the spout again.

I sighed as I changed the litter tray and opened a tin of cat food. It was up to me to do all of this as well as stay on top of my beauty therapy course. So how come Damian couldn't even keep his one, tiny room tidy? But I dared not say anything to Colin about it – he gave him a hard enough time as it was.

I was hoovering the living room when Colin came round at 9 p.m. that night, all agitated. He was chain-smoking and pacing, dropping fag ash everywhere, so I switched off the vacuum cleaner. He seemed not to notice my exasperation.

'Well, have you decided what you're going to do?' he blurted out.

I was surprised. I thought we'd already decided on a plan of action.

'Yeah, you know I have,' I told him. 'I want to get rid of the baby.'

'Get rid of it, hmmm?' he repeated this to himself as if hearing it for the first time. 'Get rid of the baby. Just like that. Is that what you want to do?'

He paused then and looked directly at me – suddenly, I felt a chill run down my spine. Something had changed since yesterday. Colin was angry now.

'This is a child from the GODS!' he erupted. 'You have been given a blessing and you want to just get rid of it? Throw it away? Like some MURDERER? Yes, a murderer – that's what you will be if you kill this child.'

He paused and I could hardly breathe, let alone speak. A few seconds passed before he carried on, calmer now: 'If that is what you want, fine. We'll do it tomorrow – but you'll have to live with that decision for your whole life and who knows how it may affect your path?'

I fell back on the sofa in despair now and, once again, I felt all my life choices being snatched away from me. The tears came easily now and I let them fall. I recalled the time I was seven years old and had wanted to run away. On the surface it looked like he was giving me the choice but in reality this was no choice at all.

He stood over me now and took a cigarette out. He lit it and blew the smoke in my direction.

'There's no point getting upset,' he said coldly. 'Just make your choice. If you want to get rid of it, we'll sort it out for you tomorrow. This is *your* path, Annabelle, *your* will. And if you choose to go against the Gods' wishes then you will have to accept the consequences, accept your path. You should just know the full implications of your decision in this matter. So, what's it to be?'

I was defeated.

From that moment I was like a zombie, completely numb inside. I could not go against the Gods' wishes; I could not kill their child. Colin said that would make me a murderer, and so I didn't have a choice. I had to have the baby. My life was not my own and I felt nothing from one day to the next. Now Colin wanted sex more often with me. He said he was getting energy from the baby inside me.

'I can see it, you know,' he told me. 'I can see the child inside you. It feeds me, it makes me stronger.'

Two weeks later, Colin called me into his living room so we could break the news to Thomas. Colin was sprawled as usual in his favourite armchair, nursing a cup of tea, a sleeping Rottweiler curled up at his feet. Thomas and I sat awkwardly on the sofa opposite.

'She's pregnant with your baby,' Colin addressed Thomas, between sips of milky tea from his Leeds United mug. 'Do you understand? You're going to be a father.'

Thomas turned to me, his face frozen in shock. I nodded at him to confirm what Colin was saying was true. He had every right to be shocked – we'd used a condom every time we'd had sex.

'But how . . . ?' his voice died away and he shook his head in wonder.

'I don't know,' I shrugged. 'I guess it didn't work one time.'

'The Gods!' Colin shouted at him, as if talking to an idiot. 'The Gods decided it for you both. At the very least you can be happy! You and Annabelle have been blessed. Chosen!'

Thomas smiled then and drew me into a cuddle.

'It's . . . er . . . it's amazing news,' he whispered into my neck. 'This is going to be great. We'll be a proper family.'

He pulled me back to look at me and then his eyes strayed down towards my stomach, where there was now the tiniest hint of a bump. I returned his smiles with my own, but they were all fake. He would never know the truth – that the baby was actually Colin's.

Hope didn't take the news half as well. She was jealous and resentful that I was going to have a kid. I suppose I was the first in our little Church group of girls who'd got pregnant. But of course I didn't want to be having a child. It wasn't my choice. It was all so twisted I wanted to scream.

But there was nothing I could do, so I just retreated further and further inside myself. By now college had finished for the summer and my placement at Julie's was over too. I didn't get out any more and I couldn't see myself returning to my course in September. What would be the point? No, my days were now spent in the house and that's all I could see for my future too: an endless round of cooking, cleaning and washing.

One day I was putting away the cutlery when suddenly my eye was drawn to a small, serrated vegetable knife with a wooden handle. Without really knowing why, I slipped it in my back pocket. Later, in the bathroom, I took it out and rolled up my sleeve. Then I pressed the blade down hard against my forearm. All I felt at first was pressure, so I pushed harder. Now the skin around the blade turned white and I started to get a tingling sensation on my arm. I felt something!

I pushed harder still and then, in a quick movement, pulled the knife towards me. I drew in a sharp breath, but it felt good. It felt like . . . like . . . something. From deep inside my shell, the pain drew me out. I saw a prickle of red dots begin to form in a straight line and I smiled. The pain, sharp and sweet, had made me feel again. I breathed hard with exhilaration and, though I knew it was probably wrong, I didn't care. I took a square of toilet paper and held it down on the gash, watching the blood seep through the flimsy white tissue. I'd found a way to break through the numbness.

The days and weeks slid past – I was oblivious to the bump above my pelvis growing steadily bigger. I didn't want to think about the baby in there; I had no emotions for it at all. Every now and then, when it all got too much and I needed to bring myself back, I'd hide in the toilet and cut myself. They weren't large marks, and I made sure I did it where Colin and Thomas wouldn't see – mainly at the top of my arm – but it felt good. I was being slowly suffocated to death and the cutting gave me oxygen. It was my only relief from the dark, heavy blanket that seemed to weigh on me at all times.

I was five months gone when Colin told me it was time to book an appointment with my GP. He'd dismissed my earlier thoughts about seeing a professional because he told me he could see the baby inside me and it was fine. I was swiftly referred to the hospital midwife who was taken aback when she found out I was so far along but I lied, telling her I'd only just found out myself. I had my first scan on my 18th birthday. As the baby's 'father', Thomas came along too – he was all excited and it was so hard to be there, pretending to share his enthusiasm.

'There! Look!' He pointed towards the screen and I forced myself to look at the indistinct black and green blobs floating in front of me. 'That's the head!'

'Do you want to know the sex?' the radiographer asked,

moving the scanner over my rounded belly.

'Yes, definitely!' Thomas answered for both of us.

'It looks like a girl to me,' she said, looking up at the screen. 'We can never be one hundred per cent certain but I'd say eighty per cent, a girl. Congratulations!'

Thomas beamed at me: 'A little girl. My little princess! Isn't that brilliant?'

I didn't think it was brilliant. I didn't think it was brilliant at all. I was devastated. In my heart I'd prayed the baby would be a boy so that Colin would never want to do things to it. A girl would be vulnerable.

When we got back later that day, Thomas went round telling everyone that I was having a girl. Colin offered his usual response:

'We knew that.'

I walked out and went home. I had to get the tea on for Moses and Olivia. Later that night, I went to my room and for the first time I let myself think about having a baby girl.

Sitting on the floor against the door, I shook my head in disbelief. I couldn't bring a girl into this situation. Would Colin do to her what he'd done to me? Would he do that to his own child? I knew he hadn't touched Hope. To him she really was his princess – he protected her from the truth about his tests and the Church. I assumed her status as his daughter assured her a place in the Palace. Would my daughter get the same treatment?

Confused and upset, I didn't know what to think. *I'm trapped.* That was the only thing I knew for certain. I was trapped in an impossible situation. *If I can't get out of this and I can't protect this child, I'll have to kill us both*, I reasoned. I slid the knife from out of my sleeve and gripped the wooden handle in my right hand, feeling along the blade with my thumb. Now I turned my left hand over to expose the creamy white skin of my wrist. I took note of the faint blue veins underneath and in a second I dug the blade in and ripped across my skin.

Instantly the blood came pouring out.

Oh my God.

It came so thick and fast, I was shocked and frightened. In that second, I knew I didn't want to die and I didn't want to kill my child. I was convinced I wanted to live more than anything else, even as the blood spurted out of my wrist and poured onto my grey leggings. *No, no no!* I gripped my wrist, pushed myself onto my feet and opened the door with my right hand, running to the bathroom. Banging the door shut with my elbow, I turned on the tap and held the open cut under cold water.

OH MY GOD!

The water stung far worse than the cut itself. It was so painful I thought I might pass out, but I managed to keep the panic at bay by focusing on my wrist and watching the water mingle with the dark blood, turning it light and pinky. After a while, I pulled it away and pressed down on it with toilet paper. I sat on the toilet then, holding it like that for ages as it bled through again and again and again, forcing me to change the toilet paper several times. I flushed each bloody wad down the toilet, trying to hide the evidence of what I'd done. I felt terrible at that moment. *I can't believe I was going to kill my baby! That would have made me a murderer.*

I stopped cutting myself after this. I knew there was nothing I could do to change my fate, so I resigned myself to my future and to the path that the Gods had laid out for me. Every day my stomach swelled beneath my clothes and I waddled after Moses as he ran from room to room, blowing me raspberries and giggling uncontrollably. He was the only person in the world that could make me feel better. The funny thing was that Colin never mentioned the cutting or the second suicide attempt. I kept waiting for him to say something but he never did. A reckless, rebellious thought began to form in my mind. *Maybe, just maybe, he doesn't know.*

Chapter 12

Damian

PEEP, PEEP, PEEP,

The insistent high-pitched beeping of my electric alarm clock invaded my dreams at 6.30 a.m. on that cold winter morning. Down on the bottom half of the bunk bed, I blinked awake and lay still for a moment. Then I stretched my limbs, being careful with the huge bump that now sat just below my ribcage. I reached out from under my warm duvet to the night-table and turned off the alarm, noting the date – 1 February. I was nine months gone now and feeling every bit of it. My due date was just days away and, although I was terrified of the coming birth, I was tired of lugging my hulking frame around.

'Olivia?' I whispered.

'Yeah, yeah, I know,' she yawned above me. 'I heard it.'

The springs from the top bunk creaked as she roused herself. I relished this extra hour I had in bed between Olivia getting up for school and Moses waking up. He slept in a cot in my mum's room but it was always me who got up with him and took him down to breakfast. I settled my head back into the pillow and closed my eyes, as I heard Olivia ease herself out of bed and walk backwards down the ladder. Then she crossed the hallway into the bathroom.

I sighed heavily. Everything about me was heavy these days – just going up and down the stairs left me breathless and sleep was now difficult to come by, as I found it impossible to settle on a comfortable position at night, cramped as I was in my single bunk bed. No sooner had I found a position that felt good than I needed the toilet. Poor Olivia was always getting woken by my nocturnal wanderings. Despite putting myself to bed earlier and earlier, I never felt fully rested these days and the morning always brought a fresh round of aches and pains.

Down the hallway I heard Damian's bedroom door open and, obviously seeing the bathroom was occupied, he crept down the stairs to the toilet. Quick as a flash, I heard his footsteps climb back up again and the door of his bedroom clicked shut. A few minutes later Olivia returned and I turned over, eager to snatch a few more minutes of sleep before the day began.

Suddenly a terrible banging and crashing started up – it came from Damian's room. I lifted my head up and Olivia and I looked at each other, confusion reflected in each other's faces.

'What does he think he's doing in there?' I spoke quietly. 'Moses is asleep. He'll wake him up. Olivia, go and knock on the door and tell him to be quiet.'

So Olivia, now fully dressed in her school uniform, walked out. I heard a brisk rap on his door, followed by a shout: 'Damian!'

At that moment everything fell quiet. Complete silence. She

came back into the bedroom and carried on getting ready while I dozed lazily.

By 8 a.m. Olivia was out of the house. Half an hour later Moses woke up, so I retrieved him from the cot in my mum's room where she was still sleeping and took him downstairs for his bottle of milk and a piece of toast. After breakfast we got dressed then I brought out the colouring pens and turned on the TV in the living room. Mum was due to go to work later that afternoon, so I knew she would want to spend the morning in bed but, as the hours passed, I wondered about Damian.

Moses proudly showed me his colouring-in – a psychedelic squirrel nibbled on a multi-coloured nut.

'Oh, that's beautiful,' I enthused, eyeing the bright pink and purple swirls on the squirrel's tail. *Waybuloo* was just finishing on CBeebies – that meant it was 11.45 a.m. Damian had to be at work at 12 noon but I hadn't heard him come out of his room since that early-morning pee in the downstairs loo. *Has he gone already?* I wondered. Maybe I hadn't heard him leave. I looked at the clock again. What if he'd fallen back to sleep? I didn't want him to be late for work.

'Moses, wait here,' I said. 'I'm going to go and see Damian. He's got to go to work today.'

Girls weren't allowed into boys' rooms and vice versa – one of the Church rules – so when I got to Damian's door, I knocked. No answer.

I don't know why but today I decided to go straight in. Normally I would wait for a response but I suppose I had a funny feeling. I turned the door handle and pushed. But it wouldn't open. There was something blocking the door – that's when I saw him, or at least, saw part of him. Damian was up against the door, sideways on, just sort of standing there, so the door seemed to stop on the side of his face. I thought he must be asleep – Damian was known for sleepwalking.

'Damian!' I said, trying to wake him up. I put my hand against his shoulder to shake him but his skin was freezing cold. Something wasn't right. He was naked. It was then I saw the belt looped over the cupboard door. My eyes went downwards and that's when I noticed that Damian wasn't standing, he was hanging an inch off the floor, suspended by the belt that was slung over the cupboard door and attached to his neck.

Oh my God!

I looked up at his face again – his glassy eyes were half-shut and his mouth hung open. There was no breath coming from his mouth at all. Damian was dead.

My heart started to pound and I shut the door as quickly as I could – then I turned round to see Moses had followed me and was standing at the top of the stairs. I don't think he saw anything, thank God, but now I was in a frenzy. A shooting pain in my belly made me wince, as I walked quickly across the landing to my mum's room.

Without bothering to knock, I went straight in.

'Mum, Damian's hanged himself!' I shouted.

Mum bolted straight up in her bed: 'What do you mean?'

'He's hanged himself in his room – he's dead. What do I do? What do I do?'

I was frantic but Mum was calm and in control.

'Go next door and tell Colin,' she instructed. 'I'll look after Moses.'

She moved like lightning, bounding out of bed and pulling on her jeans. I turned and went down the stairs as quickly as I could, grateful that someone else was taking charge. I waddled out of our back door, holding the bottom of my belly, and crossed over into Colin's garden then walked in through the kitchen.

There, I was met with an ordinary, midweek scene: Hope, Elaine, Shelley, Sandra and Thomas were all playing darts in the kitchen. For a split second I felt dreadful at the disastrous news I'd been sent to deliver. But there was no time to waste.

'Damian's hanged himself!' I announced.

The kitchen descended into chaos – Elaine, stricken, was shouting for Colin. Hope crumpled into tears and Thomas ran straight out the back door to go to our house. I just stood there, shocked and distraught. I hadn't seen or spoken to Hope in months and now I had arrived to break the news that her brother was dead. She stood in the kitchen weeping and I went to put my arms around her but she pushed me away.

'No, I can't cuddle you,' she cried. It cut me so badly, she was my best friend and she was in pain – all I wanted was to give her comfort. Elaine went to put her arm around her and Hope looked up:

'I want to see him.'

'No!' I blurted out. 'Please, please don't go up there. You don't want to see.'

Oww. Another sharp pain in my stomach took my breath

away. I had to sit down somewhere. I didn't say anything to anybody but somehow I managed to hobble back into my kitchen. Mum was waiting for me.

'I've called the police and an ambulance,' she said quietly. 'When they question you, just tell them that Damian was only staying with us for the last few days.'

I nodded to show I understood, but I didn't understand. Why did she want me to lie? By then Damian had been living in our house for well over a year. Nothing made any sense. Why had Damian killed himself? Was it an accident or did he do it on purpose?

Thomas came and sat next to me in the living room.

'I had to kick the door open,' he said, his voice quivering with emotion. His eyes bulged and his knees and hands shook. 'The belt was round his neck and attached to a crutch which he'd wedged against the cupboard door.'

'He was naked,' I breathed.

'I know.'

'Why was he naked?'

'I don't know, Annabelle. I really don't know.'

Now Colin came in the house. He looked stricken and ghostly pale. He could hardly speak at all – he just kept pacing the floor. It was the first time I'd seen him properly out of control, at a loss for what to do or say. The pains were now coming thick and fast but I didn't want to worry anyone, so I got up from the living room and went through to the kitchen, where I allowed myself to double over, giving in to the agonizing waves which now swept my body. Hope came in soon after me.

'Are you OK?' she asked. We looked at each other then, each of us hurting so badly and in that moment all the torment of the past few months just melted away. She ran to me and gave me a massive hug.

'Oh Annabelle! I can't believe he's gone. I'm so sorry I pushed you away. I need you so much.' We stood there like that for ages and then, reconciled, we waited in the kitchen together for the police to come.

'Why do you think he did it, Annabelle?' she asked me, as she stood at the back door, staring out onto the garden, where hopeful crocus heads peeked out through the frozen soil.

'I don't know,' I replied. I felt terrible, having nothing to offer her but heartache. Was he unhappy? It was so hard to tell from the little time I'd spent with him. He'd lived like a shadow in our house. I'd hardly noticed him at all.

The ambulance arrived a while later and took the body away in a navy zip-up bag. I watched them carry him out as I sat on the sofa, giving my statement to a kindly policewoman. She wanted a detailed description of how I'd found him that morning. She questioned me closely about Damian's knowledge of local news, but I didn't know the answers to most of her questions.

At this early stage, the police were linking his death to a series of teen suicides that had swept Bridgend in South Wales. Fourteen youngsters from the area had killed themselves in the previous year in a spate of what appeared to be copycat acts from Facebook – but I couldn't square this with Damian. He wasn't a teenager, after all; he was twenty-five, and he didn't even go on Facebook, as far as I knew. The police searched his room but there was no note.

Afterwards, I went in there myself with Thomas – we saw a small pile of books just in front of the cupboard door. He must have been standing on them at first like a step. Did he step off the pile voluntarily or did he slip? I wondered to myself, as I examined the area. Damian was tall – all he had to do was reach out and push himself up on one of two doorframes to save his life. He was only an inch off the ground! Why didn't he do this? Was it an accident or did he mean to die?

I couldn't begin to imagine the life he'd had until this moment. I had met Colin when I was only seven – Damian was his son, his eldest son. Colin was harder on him than on anyone else. He called him names, accused him of being 'gay' and 'dirty', things Colin equated with weakness. He belittled, humiliated and often openly attacked him in public. Had he simply suffered too much under Colin? What had he seen in those years living under Colin's roof? What secrets did he take to the grave?

That night, when Olivia came home, Mum took her aside and told her that Damian had died. Nobody told her he'd died at home, or in his room, probably at the moment she had knocked on his door. There was no point traumatizing her. It had been an exhausting and horrible day, but still I couldn't sleep that night. I spent ages on the phone with Hope, going over and over the details of the day. I couldn't bear the thought that Damian had died just a few metres from my bed, probably at the very moment I was chiding him in my head for being noisy. I felt so guilty – why hadn't I gone to check on him? Maybe I could have saved him!

'There's nothing you could have done.' Hope tried her best to reassure me. 'I mean, how were you to know what he was doing?'

'I don't know,' I said, the tears falling freely. 'I could have got up, tried to find out if he was OK.' I couldn't get that image out of my head of his face squashed up against the door, his eyelids half-open, his mouth hanging slack.

'It's late,' she went on. 'You need to try and get some sleep. This isn't good for the baby.'

We agreed to speak the next day and, at about midnight, I crawled upstairs to my bedroom – I couldn't even look in the direction of Damian's room, petrified of what I might see. I woke sometime in the early hours of the morning, desperate for a pee, but I didn't want to cross the corridor, so I lay awake for hours, unable to sleep and not willing to confront my fear of seeing his ghost. Guilt stalked those wakeful hours. *I could have saved him. Why didn't I save him?*

The next day, I was still in bits and the pains that had begun the day before seemed to be getting worse. Hope called mid-morning to invite me round to hers. I called Thomas and he came too. When we walked into the living room, I found Hope holding hands with Elaine on the sofa, who looked utterly destroyed. Colin was sprawled in his usual armchair, smoking moodily. I went to sit on the other side of Hope and she smiled, taking my hand. It was such a relief to be back as her friend, though I would have done anything at that moment to change the circumstances.

There was silence for a long time, each of us lost in our own grief. Then Colin spoke: 'I knew what he was doing.'

We all turned to stare at him now. He looked the same as ever, back in control again, but what he was saying was crazy. How could he have known?

'The Guardians told me what Damian was up to,' he went on. The Guardians were the Gods' eyes and ears on earth, apparently. It was them who watched us all the time.

'But it was his will to do it. There was nothing we could do to stop him because it was his will, his path.'

Elaine was now weeping and Hope let go of my hand to put her arms around her. I felt sick. How could he say such a thing? I knew it was rubbish – if he had known what his son was doing he would have stopped him. Of course he would! My heart went out to Elaine. How could she sit there and listen to such rubbish? If she believed him, that he had known what their son was doing, it would surely be impossible to accept the fact her husband did nothing to stop it. But then Elaine had been with Colin since she was eighteen years old and she accepted everything he said with ferocious devotion. She was his first and truest disciple. Yes, I could see she would accept this from him. She would recognize it was Damian's path, his own choice. Maybe that would make it easier to bear for her.

But I didn't buy it. I had seen Colin yesterday and, like everyone else, he was beside himself – he couldn't fake that. Once again I found myself doubting Colin's version of reality. But I didn't question him out loud – nobody ever questioned Colin. Nobody even speculated at that moment why Damian had killed himself. I was bursting with questions, tormented by my memories from the day before: a clammy, cold body and those filmy, lifeless eyes. The bare toes dangling an inch off the ground. My head swarmed with insistent questions but only silence reigned in this house.

'I know!' Colin suddenly addressed us all in an overly bright voice, slapping the arm of his chair. 'Let's have a game of darts! You know, for Damian.'

We all looked at each other and shrugged. It's true – Damian was a darts fiend. There wasn't anything else to do and it felt like some little way we could pay tribute to him.

'He did like a game of darts,' Thomas said, and smiled to himself.

'Well, come on then.' Colin pushed himself up out of his armchair, and his two Rotties got to their feet next to him. Hope helped Elaine to her feet, who appeared bewildered and upset, and I followed them all as we went through to the kitchen for a game of darts. As strange and surreal as it was at that minute, there really wasn't anything else to do.

Ten minutes into the game, Hope came across the piece of paper. She had been rummaging through the kitchen drawers, looking for something on which she could write down the scores, and now she held a torn yellow sheet in her shaking hand and her face crumpled in despair.

'What is it, love?' Elaine went to her.

'It's some scoring from another game,' Hope sniffed. 'But it's Damian's handwriting. Look!'

She showed her the note with the scrawled list of numbers.

Elaine laughed ruefully then: 'He had the worst handwriting! I can't make out anything on that.'

From where I was standing next to the kitchen counter, I could see it was definitely Damian's. His poor writing was unmistakable, and this random yet timely reminder hit me like a jolt in the solar plexus. An excruciating stabbing pain shot up my belly and I had to breathe hard. Hope was now sobbing and the sight of her so upset was awful. I wanted to comfort her but I took one step towards her and keeled over.

'Annabelle!' Elaine shrieked and ran to help me. I was crouched on the floor, my belly now spasming with hard jolts of pain. I was frightened for the baby.

'What's happening?' I panted. 'Am I going to lose the baby?'

Elaine shook her head, mute, unable to speak. Events were moving too quickly. I could see in her face she was terrified for me.

'Let's get you on the sofa,' she said softly, taking my arm. Hope took the other and, somehow, they managed to walk me into the living room and ease me back onto the sofa. The pain was now unbearable. I had spent so long trying to ignore it and hiding it from the others that when I finally allowed myself to acknowledge it, I let it take over completely. Long, hard waves of pain that started in my stomach radiated through my whole body. I looked either side of me. Elaine and Hope – the two women I loved most in the world, the ones I thought I had lost – they were here. I smiled with difficulty and Elaine patted my arm: 'It'll be OK, Annabelle – just hang in there.'

My mum appeared, and then the midwife.

I heard their voices somewhere over my head.

'She's had a terrible shock,' said my mum. 'She found the body.'

'I think it's best we get her into the hospital, get her on the monitor.' The midwife's voice was grave. 'It could be she's going into labour.'

The next thing I knew I was being helped into the passenger seat of Sandra's car.

'I don't want to go yet,' I protested weakly, pressing my fingers against the cool glass of the window. Outside, I could see Hope and Elaine standing forlornly on the pavement, holding each other, looking back at me. I wanted to be standing with them.

'I'm afraid you've got no choice, love,' Sandra replied. 'Midwife says it might be time for the baby. You've got to do what's best for the child. Now, buckle up!'

'I want to be with Hope,' I whispered, as Sandra rolled the car out of our cul-de-sac and pulled into the main road. I leaned my head back and closed my eyes. I didn't want to think about the baby. I only wanted to be with Hope.

Chapter 13

Emily

'You've got to try and relax.'

The nurse spoke gently as I clutched her hand in terror. It was my third night in hospital and a terrible storm was blowing outside. Seconds before, a huge gust blew one of the windows open and I'd screamed, petrified. Nurse Jennifer had run in, thinking it was a medical emergency. Instead, she found me cowering in the corner, crying and shaking.

'It's him!' I yelled. 'It's Damian. His spirit is in the room.'

'Annabelle, please get back on the bed,' she said, completely ignoring my insistence that a ghost was now on the ward. Although normally kind and patient, Jennifer, the nurse on the night shift, was peeved at being dragged out of the nurses' station for no reason. But I was too scared to move.

'I . . . I can't,' I stammered, crying now. 'What if he's in here?'

Jennifer did her best to reassure me, but it wasn't until she'd closed and bolted the window shut that I finally allowed myself to be led back to bed and hooked up once again to the baby monitor. I watched as the green line shot up and down erratically, my baby's tiny heartbeat reflecting the panic I felt inside.

'You've got to try and calm down,' she repeated, 'for the baby's sake. It's no good getting yourself all worked up like this. Your baby is getting distressed and that's the last thing you want.'

I couldn't speak. Inside my mind was in turmoil. I didn't want to be upset but how could I stop myself? Left alone in hospital for the past three days with no visitors, my thoughts and imagination had run wildly out of control. I was still in shock from Damian's death and all I could see, morning, noon and night, was his face. Tortured with guilt, and constantly hooked up to the baby monitor, I'd been unable to sleep properly since I arrived. Now it occurred to me the howling winds and insistent rain outside were a sign from the Gods, a sign of bad things to come.

I hardly noticed when the nurse went away and came back again, this time with an injection.

'What is it?' I asked in a daze.

'It's Pethidine,' she replied, swabbing my leg. 'It's going to help you to sleep. We know you've had a terrible shock, Annabelle, but you really must sleep, for your baby.'

I nodded obediently and let her put the injection into my leg. I wanted to sleep too but I was afraid of the nightmares, of Damian returning to haunt me. I let my eyes drift over to the monitor and watched as the beeps became slower and more regular.

'That's right, Annabelle.' The nurse was checking my pulse

now and writing things down on a clipboard at the end of my
bed. 'You just relax and try to get some sleep. It'll all be OK.'

I must have slipped into unconsciousness at some point
because the next thing I knew the light was streaming in through
the window and another, different nurse was peering down at
me, her eyes clouded with worry.

'Annabelle?' she called. 'Annabelle? Can you hear me? Are
you awake?'

I nodded groggily.

'Annabelle, you've got a slight swelling in your face. I'm
going to get the doctor. Can you sit up for me please?'

What now? It felt like everything had been fine until Damian
killed himself – now so much was going wrong. It felt like the
Gods had put a curse on me for failing to stop him dying. I didn't
believe Colin when he said that he knew what Damian was
doing, and so I doubted his idea that Damian was in charge of
his own path. I felt like I had done something terrible and now
I was being made to pay.

Hours seemed to melt away then there was more activity at
my bedside.

'It could be mumps,' the posh female doctor said to the colleague at her side. Though she was lined with age, she wore her
short, greying hair in a young, spiky style and her half-rim
glasses were attached to a funky rainbow chain. She tapped at
the clipboard with a silver pen and then peered at me over the
top of her glasses.

'Annabelle, do you know the sex of the baby?' she asked.

'Yes, it's a girl,' I replied.

'Oh, good — well that's a relief then, isn't it? Mumps can be fatal in boys, you know. We'll start you on some antibiotics.'

And with that she slid my chart back in the holder at the end of my bed and moved on.

At the next mealtime I was given my first pill — when I caught sight of it I panicked. It was enormous, the size of a grenade! I would never be able to get that down my throat. I asked the nurse if she could break it up for me and she managed to snap it into four small pieces. Swallowing each quarter, I recalled the time I took all the paracetamol. Damian's death had made me think again about the times I had tried to take my own life.

It's so selfish, I thought. Suicide is so selfish. It's a permanent solution to a problem — but what if that problem is minor or fleeting? Then you leave everyone with pain they will feel for the rest of their lives. And not just pain but real torment. All those people around you are left wondering if they could have stopped you. I realized then with certainty that if I had succeeded in killing myself it would have hurt Olivia, Moses and Hope. Maybe not my mum so much, but I knew for a fact that those three people loved me and I never wanted to bring them pain or anguish.

Why did he do it? During those long days and nights I was confined like a prisoner to that hospital bed. Hooked up to the baby's heart monitor, I turned the question over and over in my mind. He was certainly a troubled lad — how could he not be? Although Colin was careful to hide what was going on from Hope and Elaine, he certainly had no qualms about behaving in a sexual way with Millie or my mother in front of Damian. He had forced me into a relationship with Thomas. He had made me have sex with Pete. Had he done something similar with Damian before? I didn't know. So much of our lives was governed under Church secrecy, it was hard to know anything about his experiences of Colin's twisted version of religion.

All I could be sure of was that his life was intimately controlled by the Church, just like everyone else's. While he worked for a supermarket, he gave all his earnings to Colin and, although there weren't many ceremonies or meetings any more these days, he still had to stick to all the rules. Maybe when he woke up that morning he'd simply had enough? I certainly understood that. If anyone understood despair, it was me. And yet I couldn't help him. I'd lived with him day in, day out, and I couldn't help him. It tore me up inside.

By my fourth day in hospital the swelling was beginning to go down – and I had my first visitor. Thomas came to bring me a change of nightdress and underwear.

'How you feeling?' he asked, handing over a bag of clothes and some magazines.

'Not too bad,' I told him. 'How is everything back at Colin's?'

'Elaine's really cut up. They've booked the funeral now – February 14th – Valentine's Day. They all think it's a good idea 'cos that way every Valentine's Day, when everyone is thinking about love, we'll all remember Damian.'

I stayed quiet – Valentine's Day didn't mean anything to me anyway but I did wonder if it wasn't a little morbid.

'You OK?' he asked. 'They say you need to stay in now until the baby is born.'

'I don't mind,' I shrugged. 'I don't want to think about going home, back to that house. Anyway, they think I've got mumps. I'm on antibiotics.'

'Didn't you have that when you were a child?'

'Can't remember,' I replied, scratching at my palm absent-mindedly. He stayed for a short while and I spent the rest of the day dozing and reading the magazines he'd brought in.

The next morning I woke up scratching. My palms were so itchy! A couple of hours later my feet began to get itchy too. The nurse asked if I was OK.

'I'm just so itchy,' I complained. 'It's annoying.'

The doctor was called again. As she examined me, I noticed she wore cool Nike trainers under her dark trousers and white coat. This time she seemed more concerned.

'Your liver is leaking salt,' she explained. 'It's quite a rare condition and it's not generally dangerous for the mother but it can bring complications for your baby. It's probably best we induce you now, just to be on the safe side. How do you feel about that?'

'OK, if it's the best thing for the baby.'

'It really is,' she said, and now she smiled. This small, energetic older lady with her spiky hair and cool trainers – for some reason I trusted her. Most of all, I just wanted it all over with. I was sick of not sleeping, of feeling tired and emotional all the time, and exhausted with the worry. *Please get her out of me*, I thought. *Please get her out safely*.

So at 11.30 a.m. on 7 February 2008 I was induced. Almost immediately I felt an uncomfortable sensation, like I needed to go to the toilet. Then the pain came: strong, hard contractions that took over my whole body and left me limp and drained.

'I'm in a lot of pain,' I panted, when the midwife came to check on me twenty minutes later. She wheeled in a bottle of gas and air and showed me the mask. 'Put it over your mouth and breathe in deeply when you feel a contraction coming on.'

I did as she instructed and tried to use the gas and air to get control of the pain, but each contraction seemed stronger and longer than the last. Another ten minutes passed – it felt like an hour – and now I could hear myself groaning, as if from far away.

'Right, Annabelle, let's get you down to the delivery suite,' the nurse said, then she eased me out of bed and into a wheelchair.

I was still taking in big lungfuls of gas and air when we got there – a gigantic purple room with a bed and a dizzying assortment of bleeping machines. A young, black male doctor was there, as well as my midwife Helen and her trainee Emma. They helped me up on the bed and the doctor prepared a shot of Pethidine.

'What are you doing?' Helen scolded him, as he injected the back of my hand.

'It's the Pethidine,' he replied, flustered.

'No, that's the wrong needle!' she exclaimed. I could tell she was trying to stay calm for my sake, but she was still very annoyed.

I looked down to where he'd put the needle in and I could see a great big purple bruise coming up. Was it swelling up too?

'Is my hand swelling?' I asked Helen. It felt like everything was going wrong. All of a sudden, I was so scared, scared of losing the baby, scared that the Gods had put a curse on me for failing to prevent Damian's death and scared of dying myself.

'Don't worry,' she soothed, wheeling over a drip. She was just about to put it in my arm when I felt an urgent need to go to the toilet.

'I need the loo!' I shrieked. 'Can you take me please?'

'Of course.' Helen took my arm once again and led me into the adjacent toilet where I sat down and started to push.

I was straining hard when Helen put her head round the door again.

'Do you feel like you need to do a poo?' her voice rose in alarm.

'Yeah.'

'Do you feel like you need to push?'

'Yes.'

Helen looked shocked then.

'Oh dear. I think we better get you back on the bed, then. Sounds like the baby's coming now.'

'Now?' I didn't feel ready. I was frightened. There was nobody there for me except Helen and her trainee midwife. Nobody was there to calm me down and hold my hand.

'We thought it would take another few hours,' Helen puffed, as she put me back on the bed again. By now the Pethidine was kicking in and I felt so tired I could hardly move. At the same time, my contractions were getting worse. Each time they were longer and more intense and the gaps between each one were now non-existent. It was all just one long wave of agony.

'A Caesarean!' I cried out after another crest of the wave eased, giving me a brief window of clarity. I ground my teeth, feeling another debilitating pain building quickly behind the last. I spoke quickly now, knowing that in seconds my whole body would be flooded once more with unbearable pain: 'Please, please can I have a Caesarean? I can't do this any more!'

I was nothing now – I couldn't see or hear anything. All I could sense was the agony as it flowed through me. Someone tried to sit me up.

'We want to give you an epidural.' Helen's voice was in my ear. 'Can you sit up?'

I was shaking, vibrating uncontrollably and, despite having three people hold me down, they couldn't get the needle in me. I couldn't tell where I was any more – I was drifting in and out of consciousness, completely given over to the pain.

'The baby's coming!' Helen's excited voice now punctured through the haze. I was propped against the bed with my knees up but all I wanted to do was go to sleep. I had nothing left in me.

'Don't give up now, Annabelle!' Helen called over my groans. 'Your baby needs you to push. Do you want to see the head? Do you want to see your baby?'

'Yeah.' I felt so weak I could barely speak. But she heard my feeble whisper and she placed a mirror at the end of the bed. Then I managed to focus well enough to see what was going on down there. Her head! I could see a head of black hair. Suddenly, I felt a rush of emotion.

'Just one more push, Annabelle,' Helen whispered. 'You can do it. Go on!'

And so I bore down with all my might, pushing and pushing and pushing. I felt a sharp stinging pain down there but still I carried on and, with my very last ounce of energy, I pushed down.

'One more!' she shouted. 'One more!'

Gritting my teeth, I pushed again, screaming with the effort.

'The head is out,' said Helen. 'Well done – the head is out. Now take a deep breath and push again. She's just going to slide right out.'

I did as she instructed and this time it felt easier – the baby came out and, all of a sudden, they were placing this strange little creature on my chest.

Oh, my goodness! She was like a little alien – a scrunched up, creased blue face. I started laughing and crying at the same time; this was overwhelming. In that moment there was nobody else in the world, it was just her and me.

Silently, she blinked open her little eyes and looked straight at me – dark black eyes, the colour of the night. It was amazing, magical.

'Hello you,' I wept, putting a finger up to her tiny little fist, which she immediately grabbed onto. 'You don't understand how much I've been through for you!'

In that incredible first minute of her life, I was smitten. I couldn't believe how much I loved her already. For the last nine months I hadn't thought about this baby for a second. I had no feelings towards her at all. Yet, in that astonishing moment when she was placed in my arms, I fell in love. And when Helen leant in to take her off me, I wanted to stop her. *No, don't take her. Don't take her anywhere. She's mine.*

'We've got to weigh her and check her over,' Helen assured me. She seemed to read my mind. 'We won't be long. In the meantime, you've got to give me one more push for the after-birth.'

Pushing out the afterbirth actually felt soothing. I was lucky, the doctor said, that although I had some tearing down there, I didn't need any stitches. A few minutes later, Helen handed me back my daughter and, once again, my love for this tiny, helpless creature, all clean now and wrapped tightly in a white blanket, just seemed to pour out of me. Helen caught my eye and I knew then I was grinning like an idiot because she said: 'You're glowing.'

She pushed a loose strand of hair back from my face and I whispered: 'Thank you.' I was so grateful to her, for delivering my baby safely into the world; for being there for us both and leading us through this miraculous event. There was so much I wanted to say but I was so full of emotion I could barely speak.

'Well done,' she smiled. 'She's beautiful.'

'Yes, she is,' I whispered back, unable to take my eyes off my daughter's tiny little face and eyes, now closed. 'She really, really is.'

'Have you got a name?'

'She's called Emily.'

Emily. My beautiful daughter, Emily.

Chapter 14

Motherhood

*E*mily. *Emily.* I said the name to myself over and over as I stared at her through the see-through Perspex crib. Her eyes were so dark I couldn't tell where her pupils started or ended. They were like tiny chocolate buttons. *Emily.* As she lay peacefully I examined every part of her, from the tips of her tiny little fingers to the dimpled folds in her face. And, for the first time in my life, I was overtaken by an unfamiliar feeling. It was love – pure love. Around her, I felt calm and serene. It was as if the ice that had settled around my heart had melted and in its place was a new feeling: happiness.

I couldn't let her out of my sight for a moment – when the duty doctor came to check her hips, it was all I could do to stop myself leaping out of bed to punch him. The way he twirled her tiny legs around, it looked like he was going to snap her in half. When the midwife held her while I had my first bath, I was desperate to grab her back. And I wouldn't let anyone else but me give her the bottle. Colin had told me I wasn't allowed to breast-feed so I held the bottle and watched her suck greedily on the teat. *Emily.*

I laughed to myself now, when I recalled the discussions I'd had with Colin and Thomas about her name. Colin had suggested Egyptian-inspired names like Nile and Cairo – silly names that would have made her a laughing stock at school. Thomas's choices were no better, but, when I came up with Emily, it felt right. Simple, sweet and pretty; luckily, they both agreed. I looked at her now in one of Moses's old, white baby-gros and suddenly felt a surge of anger.

Why couldn't she have her own baby-gros? It annoyed me – everything I'd been given for her was a hand-me-down from Moses. This, despite the fact that I'd been given a grant of £500 to get stuff for the baby. Of course, Colin just took this money from me.

We didn't even have a car seat to take her home in, so when Thomas arrived the next day with Sandra, he had to borrow one from a friend. As soon as they got to the ward, I turned down the corners of my mouth so they wouldn't see my smile, unwilling to let them in on my newly discovered happiness. Thomas wanted to hold the baby and, reluctantly, I put her in his arms. He whisked her upwards as he proudly showed her off to Sandra and my heart lurched.

Get off her, I screamed silently. GET OFF MY CHILD!

'Ah, she looks like you,' said Sandra, admiringly.

NO SHE BLOODY DOESN'T! I had to bite down hard to stop myself hissing like a feral cat. The strength of my feeling towards my child, still just a day old, was frightening. I counted silently in my head to calm myself, as my fists balled at my side. Later, I put on her outdoor coat for the first time, then we bundled her into the borrowed car seat and drove home.

As we approached the house, I felt a knot of anxiety forming in the pit of my stomach. In the hospital, where it was just the two of us, I'd been allowed to keep an eye on my baby the whole time. There were no distractions, no people around who could cause her harm, either accidentally or deliberately. It was just the two of us and, freed from the responsibilities of the household, I'd cherished the time alone together.

Once we pulled up outside my house I felt myself becoming tense and watchful. We weren't in the house five minutes before Colin came in the back door with Hope. I was so happy to see her I grinned, but at that moment Colin picked up the car seat from the floor, with a sleeping Emily inside, and plonked it on the kitchen counter. I panicked. What if someone knocked it and she fell off? I didn't want her up there. What right did he have to come in and move her about like that? I was fuming, but of course I didn't say anything.

Instead, I turned to Hope: 'Thank you for coming.'

Hope took one look at the baby and ran out, crying. I was fed up with all this nonsense from her and for the first time I felt a power which I'd never experienced before. I raced out after her into the garden and spun her around.

'What is all this about?' I demanded. I had just had a baby, for God's sake, but she seemed to be making this all about *her*! All of a sudden, I felt strong and in control, brave even.

'It's the baby,' she sobbed.

'What about the baby?'

'She's the first Church baby,' she bawled. 'I always thought . . . I always thought it would be mine.'

'Oh, for heaven's sake!' I exploded. 'It doesn't matter that she's the first. Your child will always be more important to your dad because it will be yours. Nothing is going to change that.'

She looked at me then and in a moment I saw something else in her eyes. It was all the times she'd had to fight for her dad's attention against all the others – from my mum, Orla, Shelley, Sandra, Millie and Fiona. They were round her dad all the time now, competing for him, just the way he wanted. She had lost his attention years ago. She knew that I wasn't interested in her dad and I wanted to be her friend. Would the baby change all that? I could see the question forming behind her eyes: would the baby take me away from her?

But I couldn't even begin to go there with her – all I wanted to do at this moment was go back inside and look after my child. Out here, away from Emily, I felt panicky and out of control. I held Hope then and wiped away her tears.

'Come on,' I urged. 'Let's go in and see the baby.'

Once I was back inside, watching Emily, I felt a lot better. My mum was there, and she helped me make up a bottle, though I wasn't keen to let her feed her. That was my job.

Gradually everyone left and I took Emily upstairs to bed with me, back to my bunk bed. Since Moses was now in a cot, Emily had his old crib next to my bed. Even so, I knew this wasn't an ideal situation. Colin had promised to get me, Thomas and Emily a house of our own in the cul-de-sac – in the meantime, he suggested Olivia move into Damian's old box room and Thomas move into the bigger room with me. I didn't want to live with Thomas at all – either in this house or another. I didn't love him and he wasn't the father. The whole thing was a sham. But as I swung myself awkwardly into bed, I did feel it was strange to still be sharing a bunk bed with my little sister.

Stranger still was the thought of what had happened here just a week before. I had spent only one night in this house since Damian hanged himself and now, being back here, I was scared and uncomfortable. I didn't like the house any more. Emily and my new happiness – we were under threat in this house.

At four in the morning, Emily woke up and Mum came straight in to help feed and settle her. For the first time, she was being supportive and I wanted to say something to her, to acknowledge the way she was helping me. But I didn't know what to say. Yes, I wanted her to support me but at the same time I didn't want her anywhere near Emily. I was torn.

From the moment Emily was born, my life changed forever. It felt like I had someone worth waking up for. I loved Moses, of course, but it was different with Emily. She was mine from the start and I couldn't be separated from her for a second. The problem now was that I really resented the control Colin had over my life. It might not have been any different than before, it was just that now it affected Emily too and I hated him for it. At first, I had nothing but hand-me-downs for Emily. I didn't even have a rocker or a chair to put her in downstairs, so I used a laundry basket with an old pillow. I had to give Colin a blow job before he'd even give me the money to buy her nappies!

'I need a pram,' I told him one day. I wanted to take Emily out so she could get some fresh air.

'What do you need a pram for?' he sneered, flicking ash onto the floor.

'I need it to get her to her doctor's appointments,' I said. 'Or when I'm bringing her out with me to see you.'

'She doesn't need a pram yet,' he replied. 'She's so small you can carry her if you need to go out.'

And that was the end of the discussion so, for the first few months of her life, Emily had no pram and still no car seat. If I went anywhere in Sandra's car, I had to hold her on my lap, which I knew was illegal.

Two weeks after Damian's death, there was an inquest into how he died. My mum went along and afterwards she told me the police had found footage on his mobile of him recording himself while he was hanging, so they reckoned it had been some kind of sexual thrill gone wrong: autoerotic asphyxiation, they called it. The coroner had recorded a verdict of accidental death by hanging. So he hadn't meant to kill himself after all.

I didn't know if that made things better or worse. I mean, I had to accept the official version of events but it seemed so weird and it confirmed that he hadn't wanted to die.

I still couldn't shake the terrible guilt I felt that I hadn't done anything to stop it. Also, it spooked me out that somewhere there was a film of Damian at the moment of death. It made Colin's idea that this was his son's 'will' even more unlikely than before. I mean, clearly it hadn't been his will – it was an accident, pure and simple.

I didn't go to the funeral – nobody thought it was a good idea for me to take a newborn. Instead, I stayed in the house with Moses and Emily and, actually, alone like this with the kids, I felt good. It was the other people that bothered me. And it was due to get worse.

After two months we cleared out Damian's stuff, Olivia moved into the box room and Thomas bought a double bed and moved into my room. Once again, I was obliged to have sex with him, but only on Colin's command. He loved being around Emily so he could be her daddy but personally I found it irritating. It was almost a relief when Colin insisted he take a job in Tenby and that way he wasn't around so much.

Also after two months Colin started having sex with me again. The idea of having sex was a complete turn off for me, but now he insisted on doing it in my room while Emily was asleep in her crib. I hated that – it didn't feel right to be having sex in front of a child.

One day, after he had insisted on rough anal sex – something I hated – he told me I would soon be getting my first tattoo.

'Now that you have a child of the Gods you need to wear a symbol all the time to protect you both. That way, when you get to the Palace gates, they will recognize you as the chosen one.'

I wasn't told the design of the tattoo or even where it would be on my body. All I knew was that at some point it was coming and I needed to be prepared.

By now my body had snapped back to its original shape and I'd lost so much weight I was a size 6. The mini-skirts I had to wear at the weekends for Colin kept falling off my hips. It was the endless housework I had to do. Since Mum worked away four days a week, I was now effectively mum to three kids – Olivia, Moses and Emily – and I was constantly on the go.

Hope was still at college but in the mornings she would come and visit me and the baby and spend time with us. Luckily Emily was a brilliant baby – she slept and ate and was really content. I still yearned to finish my college course but, in some ways, motherhood really suited me. I certainly never expected to love my child in the way I did. It was a constant wonder and a delight to wake up next to her every morning. She made me happy. It was as simple as that.

One morning at 10 a.m., after I'd got Olivia off to school and I was in the living room, playing with Moses and Emily, Hope came in, closely followed by her dad.

'Are you ready, Annabelle?' he asked mysteriously.

'Ready for what?'

'Just answer me – are you ready?'

Suddenly I realized what he was talking about – it was tattoo time.

'Yes, I'm ready,' I told him. 'Can I take Emily?'

'Don't be so stupid,' he scoffed. 'You'll leave her here with Sandra.'

I didn't like that. I'd never been separated from my baby for any length of time before, and from that moment I started fretting. Would Sandra know what to do if she needed changing? I had never had a tattoo, so I had no idea how long I'd be away for.

But Colin didn't give me any time to prepare. Half an hour later, I was signing a consent form in the tattoo parlour. I didn't tell the tattoo artist that I hadn't seen the design yet. The next thing, I was taken through to the chair at the back and it was there I caught sight of the drawing on the table. It was a very large, colourful scarab beetle with outstretched wings.

Oh my God. I wanted to turn and run away right then. It was ridiculous – and huge!

'Right . . .' the female tattoo artist was pulling up a chair next to me. 'I think it's best if you take your top off altogether.'

For the next three hours I sat in the chair while she tattooed this enormous beetle on the top of my left arm. And I hated every minute. It didn't hurt that much – compared to childbirth, it was a real walk in the park. It was the fact that this was being done to me, and I didn't have any choice in the matter. Now I was branded for the rest of my life.

Colin spent the time in the bookies and afterwards, when he came to pick me up, he looked it over with a real sense of pride.

'Yes, that's good,' he said, turning my arm over to get a good look from all angles. She'd wrapped it in Cellophane to protect the skin but you could still see it underneath, huge on my arm.

'She's done it really well. This is a nice job. Isn't it a nice job?'

I had to nod but inside I wanted to cry.

'You should feel grateful to have such a beautiful symbol of protection on your body forever,' Colin told me, as we walked back that day. I was so eager to get home and see Emily that I just agreed with him all the way.

'That scarab will protect you here on earth and in the afterlife, no matter what happens in your path,' he went on. 'You have created a child for the Gods – you have brought about a renewal of life, of their life, and therefore they owe you that protection. Now they will always know that you are the giver of a sacred life.'

That night I examined my giant beetle in the bathroom mirror. Urgh. My stomach heaved. I knew for a fact I would no longer wear sleeveless vest tops in summer. It was fine for the Gods but I didn't want another living soul seeing this disgusting tattoo.

The following week, after another session of rough sex in my bedroom, Colin told me that it was time for me to start working for the Church, just like my mum, Shelley, Orla and her girls.

'Are you ready to show your devotion to the Church, to set yourself on a path to the Palace?' he asked, as he lay on the double bed Thomas had bought, stroking my scarab tattoo.

'Yes,' I replied.

'I would have sent you to work when you turned eighteen, but of course you were pregnant, so it wasn't possible,' he said, his long yellow fingernails tickling my skin. 'Now that you've recovered, it's time for you to do your duty. There are lots of different jobs you can do. One of them is to go into the film side of things, another is working in a shop and then there's the one relating to your quest to become the Whore of Babylon.

'This third one, of course, would be most relevant to your path, since it would draw you closer to the highest spiritual level needed to become the Scarlet Woman. It is, I believe, your destiny. But you have to prove it to me, to yourself. The joys of love will redeem you from all pain. Follow the ordeals of knowledge. The prophet shall reveal unimaginable joys on earth and to his woman, the Scarlet Woman, all power shall be given. Do you understand?'

I nodded, but it was a lie. I understood less and less these days of what Colin was talking about.

'Success is your proof, courage your armour. Let the Scarlet Woman raise herself in pride – let her work the work of wickedness. Let her kill her heart! Let her be loud and adulterous! Let her be shameless before all men. This is your path, Annabelle – you must inhabit the Scarlet Woman, show your power!'

On and on he went. I was hardly listening any more. I was watching my little girl sleeping. Her dreamy countenance melted my heart and inside my soul cried out, drowning his dark and twisted words: Emily, Emily, Emily!

Chapter 15

Bristol

I sat on the large double bed in the unfamiliar room, tracing the line of the pink embroidery on the black satin sheets round and round and round. *Could this be happening? Is it real?* It felt like a nightmare from which I hoped I would wake up any minute in my own bed, in my own home in Kidwelly, and see my beautiful daughter staring back at me. But no. The seconds ticked by and the room stayed the same, with me in it. I looked down at the red baby doll negligee I was wearing, the red lacy knickers and bra set and the black stilettos. I couldn't believe this was me.

Just a few hours before it had been a normal day – I was looking after Emily in the living room when Colin came striding in through the back door. He picked up Emily and immediately started bouncing her up and down on his lap – she was jiggling around uncomfortably and I wanted to say something but, of course, I kept my mouth shut. He seemed to be in a buoyant mood.

Eventually, after some cooing and tickling under the chin, he turned to me: 'Well, my little Whore of Babylon, today is the day!'

I looked at him quizzically.

'You'll be going to Bristol today with Orla,' he went on. 'Be ready for 4 p.m. and take the stuff you bought last week. Your mum will explain everything when you get there.'

I didn't even know where Bristol was – I'd never heard of it before – but I knew this was about my working for the Church.

'Who's going to look after Emily?' I asked him.

'I am!' He grinned and turned back to face her. 'It'll be fun, won't it, little one?'

My heart sank. I couldn't bear the thought of leaving Emily for any length of time, but worse, I knew Colin would make a poor babysitter. He didn't care about anybody's needs but his own. Already, I had a bad feeling about this.

'How long will I be gone?' I asked, biting down on a well-chewed nail.

'Never you mind,' he snapped back. 'You just concentrate on working hard for the Church and don't disappoint me!'

So that afternoon I got myself ready, putting all the things we'd bought into my black wheelie beauty case. I was still completely in the dark as to what I was about to do. The week before I'd been sent to Peacocks with Mum to buy some knicker and bra sets. Mum picked out a pair of red lacy French knickers with matching bra, a black thong set and a sheer baby doll negligee with lace trim at the top and bottom. It was a far cry from the ordinary white cotton I usually wore. She also chose a hold-up suspender belt in black and a pair of razor-sharp black patent stilettos.

Normally I loved shoes, and I would have been excited at the chance to wear a pair of high heels, but these weren't pretty, they were trashy. I couldn't for the life of me work out what all this was about. As she held up each set to examine them in the light and then placed them in the basket, I turned my mind off. *What will I make the kids for tea?* I wondered.

The next day she took me to Superdrug to stock up on hair and make-up products – black mascara and kohl eyeliner and red lipstick. Once again I found myself distracted, thinking about Emily and whether I was going to give her a bath that day. Mum even bought me a pair of new hair-straighteners but I hardly noticed. I didn't even think to ask her what all this was for – I knew better than that. I knew that it would all become clearer in time. For the meantime, I was happy not to know.

By 4 p.m. I was sat on the sofa in my living room, clutching Emily for dear life, terrified at the thought of leaving her. When Mum went to work for the Church it was usually for three or four days at a time – would I be gone that long? I prayed that it wasn't long and held her even tighter. It was the first time we were to be separated overnight and I was a bundle of nerves.

She only knew me! What if Colin didn't look after her properly? What if he didn't know how to change her or what time she had her nap? How would she get to sleep without me there to soothe her? I watched, as Orla ambled up the driveway, closely followed by Colin.

'Come on!' she yelled, as she rapped at the front door, making me jump. 'Let's go!'

Was this really happening? I didn't want to leave my daughter at all but I didn't have any choice. Reluctantly, I got to my feet and, as I did so, Colin came striding in the front door.

'Go on now,' he said. 'It's your time, your path, Annabelle. Go and work hard and I'll see you in a few days.'

He held his arms out so I could give him the baby but I couldn't bring myself to do it. Every ounce of my being was screaming out and I could see he was getting impatient. Nobody disobeyed Colin.

'Come on, hand her over,' he growled. 'Now.'

Still, I couldn't move. Then he barked: 'DO IT!' and I nearly jumped out of my skin.

I couldn't delay any longer, but still I had no idea how hard this was going to be. Desperately fighting back the tears, I placed her into his arms. Ripped from my warm embrace she started to cry and then, as I lingered and held my hands out towards her, she started to bawl.

I just stood there, unable to move, my heart in tatters.

'Go on, get out of here!' He jerked his head towards the door. 'Go on now. She's fine.'

But she wasn't fine. I knew she wasn't fine. She was screaming her head off and I could feel myself bubbling up with tears too. I didn't want to leave her for a second but, if I stayed any longer, it would only get worse. So I turned around and marched out of the door to the terrible wails of my three-month-old daughter, crying for her mummy.

For the next two hours I watched the motorway whizz past the window and thought of Emily. Leaving her there with Colin had been the hardest thing I'd ever had to do. I never realized until this moment just how much I needed her. And as we drove further and further away, I felt my whole world tipping on its side. She was everything to me now. She was the reason I breathed. I knew then that without her, my life simply didn't make sense.

Next to me, Orla was quiet and uncommunicative. It was hard enough to leave my home, my baby and the town I'd grown up in, but I had no idea where we were heading or what we were going to do. I was floating through the air now, completely untethered and felt very, very afraid. *Where was I going? What was happening to me?*

Two hours later we pulled into Bristol and snaked in and out of a host of anonymous suburban streets until we climbed a hill next to a house where Orla parked up. She got out her mobile phone and sent a text. A minute later, Shelley came out of the front door and Orla said to me: 'Right, you get out now and go with Shelley.'

I got out of the car and pulled out my black wheelie case from the back seat. Shelley waited while I got my stuff and then started to walk up the hill. It was around 6 p.m. now and our bodies cast long shadows on the pavement in front of us. A minute later we stopped at a shop painted pink and black. A bright neon sign above the door announced it to be The Paradise Lounge.

Shelley rang the doorbell and a woman answered. At first I thought it was a stranger but I got the shock of my life when I realized the huge bouffant hair, the extravagant eye make-up and painted nails belonged to Orla's daughter, Fiona. I actually gasped in shock!

She ushered us both inside, now wearing a sly smile as she noted my amazement at her appearance. Beneath a salmon-pink Chinese-style dressing gown, I could see she just had on a pink lacy bra and knickers and her legs were bare atop towering diamanté heels. She looked extraordinary. She led us through to a reception area where there was a black desk with two black leather chairs.

Fiona's heels clicked loudly against the terracotta tile floor, as I tried to take in my new surroundings. There was a door that led out to the back, a staircase that disappeared to another floor and, to the left, a chest of drawers with a small telly on top. Next to that, a fold-out plastic chair, a little plastic table and a sofa covered in a bright-pink throw.

'Come with me,' Fiona said, as she walked through the door to the back of the shop. Still confused, I followed her dumbly. I didn't know what we were all doing there. It was all such a mystery. We came to a room on the left side of the dark corridor. In the dimmed light, I could make out a massive mirror on the wall, a bed with black silk sheets and flowered patterns picked out in pink, and a small shelf with a box of tissues and a pack of nappy bags. Fiona kept walking up the corridor, so I followed her and in the next room I saw Millie and my mum lounging on a big double bed. Mum was also dolled up in make-up and underwear while Millie was in her outdoor clothes like me, a small bag at her feet.

This room was painted bright pink with white tiles on the floor, another big mirror on the wall and a shelf, this time with towels and a bottle of hand sanitizer and another box of tissues.

I could see a small shower room leading off to the side. The bedding was pink and silky again, embroidered with a black chandelier motif. I was intrigued, baffled and shaking with fear all at the same time. Shelley nodded at Millie, who left the room. She handed me two packets of condoms, then she left too and I stood there, staring after her, holding the packets as my mother eyed me from the bed.

'You better sit down,' she said, and I gingerly sat next to her. I was dressed in a pair of jeans and baggy striped shirt, so it felt odd to be next to my mum in her underwear. It was about to get a lot odder.

'It's like this,' she started. 'Your name here is Camilla. When a punter arrives, you go out the front and introduce yourself as Camilla and everyone else introduces themselves and then the bloke picks someone. They pay £60 – that's £30 for you and £30 for the house – and you take them up to the room. It's £60 for half an hour. For that they get a blow job with a condom, and sex with a condom, and once they come, it stops.'

My heart was racing and I felt myself breathing hard now. Strangers came here to pay to have sex with us? I couldn't believe it. Of all the things that had gone through my head about the type of work I was going to do for the Church, something like this had never crossed my mind. But it didn't stop there.

'Once they're in the room, they can pay to have extras: it's £20 for kissing, £20 for oral sex and £50 for a blow job without a condom. After each time you've got to text Colin – just say 'hello' and add either one kiss, or two or whatever, depending on how many extras they've had. You got it?'

I just nodded. I didn't trust myself to speak at this point.

'Good, because we haven't got long. Doors will be opening soon and you've got to get ready.'

The next hour passed in a blur, as Mum helped me to get ready. She picked out the red lacy bra and knickers set and I put the baby doll negligee on over the top. My fingers were trembling so much I couldn't attach the suspenders to the belt, so Mum went round hooking them all up. Then she applied some very heavy eye make-up and did my hair too, so that it was all backcombed to look huge.

Staring into the mirror, I hardly recognized myself. I looked like an auburn Barbie doll; the enormous hair, high heels and flimsy underwear all conspired to make my tiny frame look even smaller. I stepped forward in the heels and wobbled uncertainly. They were higher than any I'd worn before and I couldn't find my balance. I put my arms out instinctively and Mum grabbed my hand to stop me falling over.

We glanced then at each other, and in that moment I cried out to her in my heart: *Please don't make me do this, Mum! Please take me away from here*. But she was blind and deaf to my fear. She just raised one eyebrow and quipped: 'Don't worry – you won't be spending long on your feet!'

When the doorbell rang I nearly jumped out of my skin. Mum looked me up and down and nodded.

'You'll do,' she said. 'Now follow me and remember to smile. If you get picked, you take him into this room. Got it?'

I was so shocked and frightened at this point I was shaking but somehow I managed to totter down the corridor and out into the reception area. It was then I saw all the other girls come down from the rooms upstairs. In total there were six of us: Me, Mum, Shelley, Fiona and two others I didn't know. We stood in a little semi-circle in front of two young lads in the leather chairs. They looked like they were in their twenties and one was really quite nice-looking with floppy blond hair and big blue eyes.

He seemed more confident than the other lad and he spoke for his friend: 'My mate here wants to see someone.'

His mate now got up from the leather chair and nervously said hi – then one by one all the women said hello and introduced themselves. I was astonished when I heard the way my mum and the others purred seductively at the young boy.

'Hello there – my name is Diandra,' said my mum, one hand on her hip and the other playing with her long hair.

'Hi – I'm Nell,' Shelley pouted. The time was coming for me to speak but my throat felt so dry I thought I'd never get the words out.

Finally it came to me and I barely managed to look up, as I stammered out the name Camilla. I caught my mum's eye then and she glared at me. I knew she wanted me to smile. But I just couldn't.

The boy picked Fiona. He got his money out and handed over £60 in cash to Shelley, who put half of it in a cash register behind reception and gave the other half to Fiona. Then she led him out into the first room at the back. I was so relieved, and I was all ready to return to the bedroom where I'd been with my mum, when suddenly the boy's friend jumped up.

'Wait a sec, Camilla,' he said. It took a few seconds for me to realize he was talking to me. 'I think I'd like to see you.'

Oh my God, I was a bag of nerves, but I tried not to show it. I mean, I'd had sex before – lots of times – but this man was a perfect stranger. I had no idea what to expect. I stood fidgeting with the ribbon at the front of the baby doll negligee, as he made the cash transaction with Shelley, then I did what I'd just seen Fiona do and led him to the room where Mum had told me to take him.

I couldn't look him in the eye as I showed him into the room and closed the door behind him.

'Get undressed and lie down on the bed,' I instructed brusquely. 'Just so you know, I don't have sex without a condom, so don't bother asking.'

'All right all right,' he laughed, unbuttoning his shirt. 'It's a fair cop, love, you've got me banged to rights. I won't ask. Can I ask you one thing, though?'

'What?'

'What in the hell is a nice girl like you doing in a place like this?'

If I wasn't so terrified at that moment, I would have smiled. I'd been thinking the same thing. Instead, I told him: 'I'm funding my way through beauty college.'

'Really? Are you a beautician, then? I knew you were too good to be here. I wasn't going to pick anyone tonight but you changed my mind. You're stunning!'

I blushed, then turned away. Nobody had ever spoken to me like this before and, while the whole thing was dreadful and shocking, I couldn't help feeling flattered too.

'I'm not a beautician yet,' I told him. 'I've still got a couple of years to go.'

'Well, now, how 'bout a massage then, Camilla?'

'OK.' Relief flooded through me. In some ways I just wanted to get this over with – but on the other hand, the more we talked, the more he was putting me at ease.

I sat astride his back as I moved my hands up and down his spine, pressing hard with my thumbs along the ridges of his muscles.

'What's your name?' I asked.

'Mike,' he murmured into the pillow. 'Oh wow – that is really good. You have talented hands, lady! I could get used to this.'

At that moment, it occurred to me: I was on my period! I had to somehow get rid of my tampon before we had sex.

'Just wait here a minute,' I replied. 'There's no rush.'

I jumped off the bed and went into the little shower room where I'd put my beauty case and, with my back to the door, I quickly whipped out the tampon and put it in a bag. Then I went back in and carried on the massage.

After ten minutes, he spoke: 'All right, Beautiful. You've had your fun. I think I'm ready to touch you now.'

He turned over and I did as I had been instructed. I put on the condom, gave him a blow job with it on and then we had sex. The whole time, I felt nothing. It was just sex with another person; he could have been anyone.

'You know, I really hope you get your qualifications quickly,' he said, as he pulled on his jeans afterwards. 'I don't think it's right you should be here.'

I smiled sadly at him. What was there to say? He had just paid to have sex with me. Places like this wouldn't exist without people like him! I felt disgusted – with him, myself, the whole sorry state of things.

'Camilla, I'll come back and see you,' he said, as he left. 'You're lovely. You really shouldn't be here.'

Then he closed the door and he was gone. I sat there on the bed, tracing the patterns of the chandeliers on the sheets, wondering if all this was real.

That first night, I had eight clients in total. Each time I was given my half of the money and I had to invite the men to buy extras in the room. After each one, I texted Colin 'hello'. After Mike, the rest merged into one another. The long night dragged on and, each time the doorbell rang, I lined up with the other women, silently praying not to get picked.

Depressingly, it never worked. I got picked more than anybody else. The last one came in at about 4 a.m. and by then I was exhausted and hungry. I managed to grab a few hours' sleep then and, when I woke up, Mum passed me a Pot Noodle and showed me a kettle where I could fill it up. Since The Paradise Lounge was open 24 hours a day, we weren't really allowed to sleep while we were there, so we passed the time watching TV and doing each other's hair and make-up.

By midday the clients were ringing the doorbell again, and from then on it was a steady stream until Sunday morning. When Orla drove me back to Kidwelly late on Sunday morning, my black case was bulging with cash. It was more money than I had ever seen in my life – hundreds and hundreds of pounds. But all I could think about was Emily. I was missing her terribly and was desperate to see her again.

When I got home I raced in the front door, scanning the front room, calling out: 'Emily! Emily!'

Nothing. My heart was in my mouth as I ran from room to room, shouting her name, panic rising like bile in my throat. Anxiety, fear and exhaustion all threatened to overwhelm me when Mum dragged herself in the front door and yelled at me: 'Stop making that racket. She's round at Colin's!'

Heart thudding in my chest, I flew out the back door and barged into their house. I heard my daughter crying and I found her in a cot in the living room, in a state of near hysteria. The moment I picked her up she calmed down, but then I noticed the bruises and I started to shake. There were little marks on her face and neck, like someone had pressed too hard. With big fingers.

I felt her nappy – it was full to bursting, like it hadn't been changed in hours. I couldn't see or hear anyone in the house. I whisked her back home and took her up to our bedroom. I didn't want to leave her ever, ever again.

When I changed her, I saw her bottom was red and sore from being left in a soiled nappy for so long. 'I'm sorry,' I whispered into her neck, as I held her close to me that night. *I'm so sorry. Don't worry. Mummy's back. Mummy's here. I'll never leave you again.*

Sadly I was to break that promise, over and over and over again.

Chapter 16

318, 618, 918

My life took on a new nightmarish reality. I was a mum at home to my daughter during the week and, from Friday to Monday morning, a prostitute in Bristol. Colin explained that I had to prove myself worthy of becoming his Scarlet Woman by inhabiting the role of the Whore of Babylon. The numbers were laid down in the three chapters in *The Book of The Law* to represent each new spiritual level – these were 318, 618 and 918. This meant I first had to sleep with 318 men, then 618, and finally 918, to achieve the highest spiritual level. That was 1,854 men in total.

I had to keep a tally on my phone every time I had sex with someone new and keep tabs on where I was in my quest. All the girls had to do the same – we were all in competition with each other in this way and the animosity between us all grew each month.

It killed me every time I had to leave Emily. I would dread Friday coming round and then, when it did, and I had to leave her with Colin, Orla or Millie, it was awful. The whole time I was in

Bristol, the whole 72 hours, all I could think about was my daughter, wondering and worrying about what was happening to her while I was away. Each hour we were apart felt like a lifetime.

From the very beginning it was clear I was getting picked more than any of the other girls. On more than one occasion, men would be standing looking at the others in reception and then I would come out last and I'd hear them say: 'Cor, that's a bit more like it!' It was the last thing I wanted, of course, but it meant that I was earning a lot of money.

For every twenty men that walked into The Paradise Lounge, I was usually picked by twelve of them. After a while I started to get 'regulars' too – the ones who insisted on only seeing me. And many of them were rich, tipping me an extra £50 just because they'd enjoyed themselves. It meant that from Friday afternoon to Monday morning I was busy. The only time I slept was a couple of hours around dawn, so, by the time I crawled home on Mondays, I was completely exhausted.

Now I was earning up to £1,200 a night, which meant I'd come back from a weekend away and hand over £3,000 straight to Colin. A brick of cash! The next day I'd have to give him a blow job to get nappies for Emily. Something wasn't stacking up – my heart was torn to shreds, I was exhausted killing myself to earn thousands for him each week and I still had to beg for a few nappies. I could see where the money was going; Colin was busy doing up his house with plush new carpets, chandeliers, fitted furniture in the kitchen and bedrooms and buying expensive holidays for himself.

When Hope passed her driving test, he bought her a brand

new Peugeot convertible. And he'd even substituted his Umbro trainers and tracksuits with Nike.

I'd watch her driving around in her smart red Peugeot and I'd seethe with anger. *I bought you that*, I'd think to myself. I bought it by getting fucked by strangers! But, no – Colin insisted the money we gave him went straight to the Church.

'I thought *you* were the Church,' I challenged him one day.

'No, no, no,' he shook his head, smiling at my supposed stupidity. 'The Church has an international headquarters, that's where all the money goes. It's in a small town in France – you wouldn't have heard of it and, besides, the precise location is governed under Church secrecy. Needless to say, they are very happy with you.'

I was beginning to doubt him more and more now – was this really about me and my path to the Palace, or was it just about the sex and the money? I struggled to believe this stuff about an international HQ in France.

As time wore on, the work got harder and more exhausting. Colin insisted I should be an 'all-round whore', which meant offering a wider variety of services. Now he wanted me to offer anal sex for £80 a go, and he said I could charge another £30 for the customer to 'come again' within their allotted half an hour. But the worst, and the one which I couldn't accept, was charging £100 to have sex without a condom.

'What if they've got something?' I objected, when he first suggested it.

'Don't worry,' he laughed. 'The Gods will protect you. Your scarabs will protect you.'

Colin had given me a gold necklace with a scarab beetle pen-
dant after my first week as a prostitute. He said each scarab
offered a new level of protection, but now I couldn't swallow
this answer. Not wearing a condom? It was like playing Russian
roulette with my health. I told him I would offer it but, in truth,
I only did it once. If I had a million scarab beetles on me, I
wouldn't have done it twice. I was too scared. In these small
ways, I started testing Colin.

How much did he really know? I had always been fearful of
the Gods and the Guardians watching me when he wasn't there,
telling him things he couldn't see. The way he knew about the
packet of paracetamol I'd taken that time I tried to commit suicide – I saw it as evidence of his powerful reach. The way he
claimed to 'know' things before being told them. Now I tested
this for the first time by going against his wishes. And strangely
enough, he never found out.

Week after week, I slept with men of every age, race, class
and type: short and fat, tall and ugly, handsome, rich, poor,
clean, dirty, drunk, stoned, high, old, young, black, white, Asian,
Chinese, Indian, confident, shy, funny, stupid, mean, happy,
bold, obnoxious and plain old horny. And despite everything it
was an eye-opener. Over and over again, men asked me what
the hell I was doing there. I trotted out the line I'd first dreamt
up with Mike – that I was funding a beauty course, but over time
this wore thin.

'You're too good to be here,' they insisted. And after a while
I started to believe them. *What was I doing there?* I was young,
eighteen, good-looking (according to many of them), bright,

with my whole future ahead of me. I wasn't a drunk, a drug addict or homeless. Why was I there?

It was Mike who built up my confidence more than anyone. He sought me out over and over again; even when I was moved to another brothel in a different part of the city, he came and found me. He'd pay just to sit and talk with me. He wanted to take me away, for us to start a new life together.

'I can't do it, Mike,' I'd tell him. I had come to look on him as a friend, and though I didn't reveal anything about the Church or Colin, I trusted him enough to tell him I had a child waiting for me at home.

'She can come too,' he insisted. 'You've got to get out of here. This isn't the place for a girl like you. You are worth so much more and have so much to offer. I know you don't like it here, I know you don't want to be doing this. Let me support you for the rest of your beauty course until you are ready to become independent. This is no way to start your life; this is no way to raise a child. Please, *please* let me help you.'

Of course, I had no choice but to refuse but it made me think.

For the first time I was coming into contact with men who were different from Colin. Men with proper jobs, who told me about the outside world. They didn't talk about Gods, Palaces, Paths or the Abyss the whole time. Was there more to life than this? Could I start to hope and dream of building a life beyond the Church and Colin? As the months passed, it felt like I had no life at all. During the weekend I was Camilla, the prostitute. Then I'd go home and I'd be a mum, as well as Colin's sex slave.

Where had Annabelle gone? Where was me? I was a machine with no identity of my own.

The one that kept me going was Emily. She was the only light in my life and, every time I had to leave her, I became angrier and angrier. I couldn't hide it any more. I didn't even have it in me to pretend to Colin that I liked it, that I wanted to be his little whore. I just wanted the whole thing over with. Perhaps he sensed this and that's why he started buying clothes for Emily of his own accord. But it made no difference. I was in hell, he was living like a king, and the truth about the world outside was seeping into my consciousness: men weren't like Colin. *No one* was like Colin and, perhaps, the world outside wasn't as scary as he had always said it was.

In fact, I met a lot of very nice men, respectable men with good jobs who treated me well. Aside from the fact that they were paying to have sex with me, they were good, kind people. I saw men from every walk of life and most of them were nicer to me than Colin. They paid me compliments, told me I was beautiful, said I had a lovely manner, a pretty smile, a gorgeous body . . . it went on and on.

I'd never heard any of this before. Of course, it wasn't all rosy – far from it! There were the pissheads who'd try to take advantage of you, the cokeheads who took forever to come and then the rough ones who would try to throw you about. On these occasions I'd have to bang on the floor to signal I was in trouble and the other girls would come rushing in. My mum could be intimidating but it was Shelley who got really tough with the tricky customers.

But it was rare to have to summon the other girls. Usually, if you were firm but not rude to the customers, they were fine. Besides, there was precious little solidarity between us girls any more. The competition between us all was now so fierce and severe that we rarely talked. Everyone was aiming for the same thing – to get their numbers up to 318, 618 and then 918. And since I had started, most of the girls' customers had dropped off. I suffered their hateful looks and bitchy asides and I just wanted to scream: *I don't care about any of it*. All I cared about was being apart from Emily. All the time I was in the brothel, I thought about her. I was missing everything to do with my daughter growing up and it destroyed me.

When Orla wasn't driving the rest of us up and down from Bristol, she would look after Emily and now she began to tell me things about her like she knew her better than me! Worse, she crawled for the first time with her and then she told me she was standing up on her own. I was missing my own daughter's childhood – I was losing her, just like my mum lost Moses. I hated it. I hated every minute.

The turning point came in December, six months after I started working as a prostitute. It was the early hours of a Sunday morning and Mum had a regular wealthy client, a professional man named Clive, who liked to get two girls together. Usually, he chose my mum and Shelley. This night they were upstairs together for about ten minutes before Mum clumped downstairs in her heels to where I was watching TV with the others in reception. By now, the only girls who worked in The Paradise Lounge were us from the Church. It was ironic really – the brothel was full of devout Church members, working towards saving their souls in the afterlife.

'Camilla!' Mum used my brothel name when we were working. 'He wants you as well!'

'What?' I didn't like the sound of this. I never usually worked with any of the other girls – it wasn't something I was keen on – and had never joined my mum in a room before. Suddenly I felt awkward and uncomfortable.

'Come on!' Mum yelled, as she turned and stomped back upstairs. As usual, I had no choice. Mum outranked me in the Church and I knew there would be consequences if I didn't do as she said, so reluctantly I followed her upstairs.

When I got into the room, I was met by a scene I felt no wish to be part of. My mum was sat backwards on Clive, riding him and giving Shelley oral sex at the same time. I had no idea what to do with myself, so I just sat down next to them on the side of the bed. I didn't move, I didn't get involved at all and, after a while, it was all over. I was so relieved when it finished and I had managed to avoid actually doing anything that I left pretty sharpish.

But ten minutes later, after Clive had dressed and left, Mum came to me in the bedroom where I was reapplying my lipstick.

'He's just going to get some more cash then he's coming back,' she said, pulling her blue robe around her and tying the belt. I didn't know what to say to this – perhaps she wanted me to be happy for her that she was doing so well tonight. These days she was rarely picked and she could sometimes go the whole night without seeing a single punter.

She lit a cigarette, watching me as I examined my face in the mirror. Then, as she exhaled, she dropped her bombshell: 'When he gets back he wants us two together.'

Oh God. I froze. At that point I knew there would be no sitting on the side of the bed, watching. I would have to get involved, with my mum! Of course, the client had no idea we were related, not that I think it would have made much difference to him.

'I've just got to double-check things with Colin first,' Mum said, then pulled her mobile phone from her robe pocket and started texting.

I sat on the bed, staring silently at the wall. I couldn't believe what we were about to do. Things had gone too far now. I mean, what next? I sat like that for ages, just staring at the wall while Mum smoked and paced up and down, waiting for a reply. I knew already what the response would be. He'd agree – of course he would. Colin only cared about the money. That was clear to me now.

An hour later and I was lying on my back, staring at the ceiling, while the bloke kneeled in front of me and I gave him oral sex while Mum did the same to me. It was rotten. All of it. The whole thing was bloody rotten. As I lay there in that vile room feeling wretched, depraved and sickened, I resolved to get away.

I can't do this any more. I can't do this, I told myself. There has to be another way for me. *There has to be a way to live my life with my little girl without putting myself through this hell.*

From that moment I knew I had to escape. Colin would never let me just walk out and, even if I reached the target number of

1,854, there was no guarantee he'd let me stop working. I was such a good earner for him and he had got used to easy money. My mum, with a three-year head start on me, had already reached the target figure and she was still at the brothel every weekend. There would always be another level, another test. There was no way out. But I didn't for a moment consider suicide this time. I would never leave my daughter without a mum.

Just seeing her little face crumple in anticipation of my going away every Friday was enough to make me scream with the injustice of it all. I could have ripped Colin's face off then with my bare hands. The ferocity of my anger was overwhelming. I was more than his little whore, more than Camilla the prostitute. I was a mother! Why did he have to take my daughter from me? Why did he tear my heart in two like this? He had forced me into the situation. He had insisted I have his child. Now I was at breaking point – physically, mentally and spiritually. I couldn't go on like this any longer. I couldn't take any more. And I couldn't put my daughter through such pain.

I had to make a plan.

Chapter 17

The End

The first thing I did was take money. Well, it wasn't really stealing since it was money I'd earned myself, but at the end of every weekend, instead of handing everything over to Colin, I'd keep a little aside for myself. It was very risky. If any of the other girls had seen what I was doing they would have told him and I'd have got into trouble. Usually I handed over my wad of cash in a large pink purse he'd given me exactly for this purpose. I kept my secret stash hidden away in a zip pocket of my beauty case that was tucked behind a little flap of black fabric. If you didn't know the zip was there, you wouldn't think to look.

At first I only held back a small amount at a time – £30 or £40 from one extra I'd earned in the room that I didn't tell him about. I was testing him. Could he tell I hadn't given him the money? Did he know when I was deceiving him? After a few weeks, and no comeback, I got bolder. Now I held back £200 a time and he still didn't notice. No, he didn't have eyes in the back of his head, he wasn't all-powerful. So I took money for myself every week and slowly my escape fund began to grow. This was my way out, the key to getting away from Colin for good. I realized that if I wanted to leave and survive on the outside, I had to be able to stand on my own two feet financially.

Next I enlisted Thomas. Thomas was still living in my house but he too was increasingly unhappy with the arrangements Colin had made for us. He knew nothing of the brothel and the 'work' we all did in Bristol – this was governed under Church secrecy, of course – but he was dissatisfied with being sent to Tenby. Most of the week he was up early to get to work on time and back late, meaning he spent very little time with Emily. Worse, at the end of every week, he had to hand over all his hard-earned wages to Colin. For the first time the Church rules riled him.

'Why can't I keep my own money?' he stormed one night. 'I want to provide for my own kid. I want to buy her nice clothes. I'm working all the bloody hours but what's the point if I can't even treat her to something nice at the end of it all?'

'If we get away from here we can finally be together as a family,' I told him. 'We can be free of the Church and all the rules. It's time we lived our own lives.'

'It's what I want,' he whispered earnestly. He was terrified Colin would hear him through the walls. So many years in this twisted community had taught him never to trust anybody and always to watch your back. Now, however, he'd finally had enough.

'But how can we do it?' he asked.

Poor Thomas had even less confidence in his abilities to go it alone than me. For a while I'd been thinking about how to get away and one thing that occurred to me was that we'd need help from outside. I'd been mulling this over for a while and finally it was time to put my ideas into practice.

'Remember Alan? My mum's old boyfriend?'

'I think so – nice guy. Bald. Big belly?'

'That's him. Well, we always got on really well. He was more like a dad to me than anyone else, but then, when we came here, he got pushed out by Colin and the Church. I think he would have stayed with us but Mum didn't want him around any more. Anyway, I know he'd help me if he thought I needed it. Can you go to the library, use the computer and see if you can find him on that thing? Facebook, is it? If you find him you can ask him to help us. He can drive. If he agrees, then we'll be able to get out of here safely.'

So, in early January 2009, Thomas began his online searches and it wasn't long before he came up with the result.

'I've found him!' he whispered one night when we were alone in the bedroom. 'He's in Carmarthen, only about half an hour away. He says we're more than welcome to stay with him and his wife for as long as we need to. He wants to see you, Annabelle. He says he always knew this day would come.'

I sat back in bed, astonished. I couldn't believe the plan had worked so easily. So smoothly.

'When can he come and get us?' I asked Thomas.

'Whenever you want – you just have to name the day.'

I couldn't believe it was all so easy. Despite my exhaustion that night, I lay awake for hours, thinking about Thomas's news. Alan had been half an hour away all this time and he'd never come to see me? Of course I was pleased that he had responded to my cry for help, but I couldn't help feeling hurt and abandoned by the man I had once looked on as my dad in all but name.

Where were all the people I'd known before Colin and the Church engulfed me and my family? Where was Alan, my grandparents, my aunts? We had come up to Wales and, within a very short time, everyone I'd known before had vanished. My grandparents came to see us just once and my aunts didn't come at all. They'd never even met my brother Moses. I wondered how it had come about. I knew my mum had pushed people away. Even so, there were no calls, no birthday cards, nothing. Now I felt as far away from my old life as it was possible to be. What was there for me on the outside?

I wondered and worried in this way for hours. Every time I closed my eyes a fresh question popped into my head and, though my whole body ached from tiredness, my mind was a whir of activity. Finally, wrecked with fatigue, and just as the sun came peeping through the curtains, I managed to drop off for a short while.

For the next few days Thomas and I discussed the best way forward. We both agreed the pick-up would have to be in the early hours of the morning, when no one would be around, preferably a Friday morning. In the past two months, Mum had started going to work on Thursday nights. But we couldn't leave Moses and Olivia alone in the house, so the plan was that I would escape first with Emily. Thomas would stick around to watch the other two and then he would tell Colin that I'd done a bunk in the middle of the night, claiming to be completely ignorant of my plan. A few days later, he would come to us directly from work.

'How do you think he'll react?' I asked Thomas nervously. I feared he wouldn't be able to pull it off. Could he lie convincingly to our Church leader, the man he'd admired and respected his whole life? What if Colin didn't believe him?

'Who knows?' Thomas replied. 'I mean, he won't like it but knowing him, he'll say he saw it all coming anyway!'

'My path!' I laughed.

'Your path to freedom, more like,' he countered.

We laughed and talked excitedly, though underneath I didn't feel quite so brave. We set a date – it was to be 13 March at 2.30 a.m. Alan would park at the top of the cul-de-sac, so that nobody would be woken by the sound of his engine. As the day got nearer I counted and recounted my money: £1,600. Was it enough? How far would I get with £1,600? How long would it last? I worried about Thomas – some part of me still didn't trust him. I knew that he was arranging the escape, but what if nerves got to him? What if he cracked and told Colin where I was staying? Colin was so clever at twisting things – Thomas had to be very strong to stand up to him.

But, most of all, I was frightened of leaving the Church, Colin, my mum and the security of everything I'd known in my life until this point. Colin had always warned me about leaving; he told me that without the Gods on my side, I'd be unprotected. I would be at risk of bad things happening. Now his words came back to me, I felt paralysed by his dire warnings: I would be putting my daughter in the path of danger. What if I couldn't support us? What if Alan let us down or threw us out – who would we turn to?

Without Colin and my mum, I really had nobody. Finally, I was devastated at the thought of leaving my sister and Moses. That was too hard. Moses thought of me as his mother – who would love and care for him like I did? What chance did he have without me?

A day before the arranged escape, I pulled out.

'I can't go through with it,' I told Thomas tearfully that night. 'I'm not strong enough. Tell Alan it's off.'

'Are you sure?' Thomas couldn't believe it. The whole idea had come from me; I was the one who had given him courage and now I was falling apart.

'Yes,' I sniffed. 'It just doesn't feel right. I don't know why, I really don't. Just please, call Alan and tell him it's off. For now.'

'Really?'

'Yes, really. I can't do it!' I repeated sharply. I wanted to leave so much it hurt. But at that very moment, I just couldn't do it.

The next few weeks I was more depressed than I'd been in my whole life. To come so close to escape and then bottle it at the last moment – it was devastating. I'd let my daughter down again. The next Friday night I had to leave Emily was an unbearable wrench. *This shouldn't be happening*, I berated myself, as I turned to leave, her little face crumpling in sorrow once more. *We should be gone by now.*

Later, I lay on my back in the brothel as strangers pummelled me again and again, the same words spun round and round in my head: *this shouldn't be happening. It shouldn't be happening . . . shouldn't be happening.* It was all I could think about.

I was so ashamed I'd lost my confidence at the last minute but, at the same time, I knew that this wasn't over. One day, I would escape, I told myself. One day I would be ready. After all, I still had the money. In fact, I was collecting more than ever before. I'd decided £1600 just wasn't enough money to survive, so now I was taking £300 or more each weekend, and still Colin didn't notice.

The truth was, it wasn't so easy to leave my family – yes, it had been simple enough to put in place the arrangements for escape, but how ready was I to turn around and walk out on Olivia or Moses? He was practically my son – I had raised him! Now I had to leave him, possibly forever. It tore me up inside. If there was any way of taking him with me, I would have tried.

But no matter how much I turned it over in my mind, I knew I had to leave him. He wasn't my child. If I took him with us it would be kidnapping and then Colin would call the police and I would be putting my daughter in jeopardy.

No, I couldn't take him. So, over the next few weeks, I saved my money and silently said my goodbyes to my siblings. I held Moses tighter than ever, I played with him longer, I kissed him more often. I tried to give him all the things he would miss when I was gone.

Two months after I backed out of the first escape plan, I told Thomas I was ready to go. And this time, I was sure.

'Hush, honey-pie,' I soothed, as I picked up a sleepy Emily and wrapped her snugly in a soft fleecy blanket. It was 2.30 a.m. on 22 May and I hadn't slept a wink all night. I'd gone to bed the previous evening next to Thomas, fully dressed in my jeans, wearing four pairs of knickers and five T-shirts. Since I could only take my beauty case, there wasn't much room for my clothes, so I wore as many as possible.

The bag had been packed and ready to go since early evening – inside were Emily's clothes, some nappies, her red NHS book and my passport. Apart from that, I also had £3,000 zipped into the little pocket at the back. Thomas had been dozing lightly when I told him I was about to leave. He opened his eyes groggily and yawned, stretching out both arms. How can he be so relaxed? I wondered. I was a mess of jangling nerves.

'It's going to be fine,' he whispered. 'Don't worry, we'll all be together soon.'

I smiled weakly, terrified that at any minute we might be discovered; petrified in case the plan didn't come off. I said goodbye – no kisses or hugs. It wasn't like that between us. We just nodded solemnly at each other, then I closed the bedroom door behind me.

I wheeled my little suitcase out of my room, being careful not to step on the creaky floorboards. I didn't want to wake up Olivia or Moses. I paused briefly on the landing and looked at their closed doors; behind each was a sleeping sibling whom I was leaving behind. In my heart I sent them a silent message: *I love you and I'll do my best to come back for you. Until then, be strong, be clever and survive.*

I blew one last kiss in the direction of each child, then I tiptoed downstairs to the dark living room, Emily curled up in her blanket and asleep on my shoulder. I pulled out the envelope I'd prepared earlier. Inside was the chain Colin had given me with the scarab beetle and on the front I'd simply written 'Colin'. This I placed on the kitchen counter. I took one last look around at the still and silent house, the place I had grown up and spent so many miserable years, and carefully opened the front door.

Outside, the road was quiet and misty, the fog catching an orange glow from the streetlamps. I knew this would be the most dangerous part, getting away from my own front door and past Colin's house. I felt myself shaking with fear, as I placed one foot in front of the other, my heart nearly bursting through my chest. I had just got to the end of the front path when one wheel of my beauty case caught the kerb and fell awkwardly onto the road, making a clunking noise that punctured the night's silence. I froze, my eyes darting anxiously upwards to Colin's bedroom window.

It was slightly ajar, thanks to the warm weather, and I prayed that the curtains would stay closed and the room dark: *please stay asleep, please stay asleep, please stay asleep*. My head was ablaze with terror and alarm but, on the outside, I was still, like a statue. I waited there like that, holding my breath for what felt like an eternity. It was no more than seconds but then, when I realized there was no reaction, I let out my breath and started walking again. Now I crept as quietly as possible past each of the houses in the street, every sense alive to the sounds and movements around me.

As soon as I was round the bend in the top of the road, I saw Alan in his car – he looked exactly the same as he did from all those years before – and his face cracked a wide smile when he saw me. I wanted to smile back. I was so relieved to see he was actually there waiting for us – some small part of me had worried he might not be there at all – but I couldn't smile at that moment if my life depended on it. My heart was being ripped to shreds. I couldn't bear the thought of leaving Moses and knowing that I might never see him again. I walked quickly now towards the car and Alan got out to meet me.

'Hello, babe,' he whispered, as he took hold of the beauty case and put it on the back seat. Next to that was a car seat for Emily. He took Emily off me gently, being careful not to wake her, and deftly strapped her in. I jumped in the passenger side and almost immediately erupted into sobs.

'Please let's go,' I said, shaking and crying uncontrollably.

'OK, OK – we're going,' he assured me, as he started the engine and backed out. Then, in another second, he'd pulled away and we were heading through the empty streets, out of Kidwelly.

For the first ten minutes I couldn't speak.

'Are you OK, love?' He put his hand on my shoulder when we stopped at a traffic light and we looked at each other then, properly, for the first time in years. His soft, kind eyes were so familiar, so reassuring at that moment.

'Yes,' I sighed, dabbing at my eyes with a tissue. 'Yes, I'm sorry, Alan.'

'Hey, there's nothing to apologize for. I'm just so glad you made it.'

'It's good to see you.' I finally smiled through my tears.

'Good to see you too.' And with that we were away again, driving northwards, moving further and further away from Colin, my mum, the Church, my family and home.

As the miles disappeared behind us, I looked back at my daughter, still sleeping soundly. All this had been for her. Just looking at her gave me strength and hope, and I took comfort from the fact that I knew this journey was the first step in giving her a good life.

After half an hour we pulled into a small street and alongside a big house.

'I live here with my wife Leah and our son,' Alan said quietly, as he opened the front door, swinging in the car seat behind him.

'She knows all about the situation. She says you're more than welcome to stay for as long as it takes for you to get on your feet. I've told her a little about the Church, so she understands.'

Alan knew Colin was in charge of the Church, but to him it was all just meetings and meditation. He knew nothing of the 'work' we had all been doing in the name of the Church. It crossed my mind that I had started working as a prostitute in June the year before and now, a little under a year later, I was on the verge of completing my quest. According to the tally on my phone, I'd slept with over 1,800 men. I shook my head. I couldn't think about that right now. All I said was: 'That's kind of her.'

I was exhausted. I had spent so much time and energy planning for this moment and slept so little in the past week, I could barely keep my eyes open. The hallway was dark and silent – everyone was in bed. It was frightening to be in a new house in a whole new town, but even the fear wasn't enough to stop my eyelids sagging. I couldn't hold back the fatigue that was dragging me down towards unconsciousness. I'd had enough – my brain needed to switch off. Alan led me to a sofa where I curled up next to Emily under a big flowery duvet and immediately went straight to sleep.

Chapter 18

Life on the Outside

I awoke to the sound of my daughter's giggling. She was lying next to me, playing with my face, squashing up my nose and cheeks and laughing. I opened one eye and she giggled some more. Then I pretended to go back to sleep and, when she poked my chin, I opened both eyes wide and looked straight at her. She laughed with surprise. I closed my eyes once more and this time she put both chubby little hands against my cheeks and held my face.

It was such a simple, beautiful gesture I felt like crying. Instead I kept my eyes closed and, just as she started to wonder whether I was asleep again, my eyes sprang open and I whispered: 'Boo!'

She squealed and erupted into another round of giggles. This was what it was all about. This was the reason I was waking up on a sofa in a strange house in a town I didn't know. In that moment I thought about the house I'd left behind – what would be happening there now? How would Colin take the news of my disappearance?

Rubbing my eyes, I sat up and took in my surroundings – the furnishings were simple but elegant. Emily and I were sprawled on a huge, grey corduroy sofa which was pushed against plain white walls on a stripped wooden floor. There was a TV at one end of the room and an assortment of family pictures on the wall behind us.

I studied the pictures, searching hungrily for clues of the life Alan had carved out for himself after us. There was a picture of a young boy, around three years old, hanging off a playground roundabout, grinning. Another one of Alan with a tall blonde woman, both smartly dressed as if for a wedding. She wore a silky powder-blue dress with a sweetheart neckline and a feather fascinator; he was in chinos with a smart, buttoned-up denim shirt. They both looked so happy. For a moment I felt horribly envious.

'Morning!' Alan popped his head round the door. 'Cup of tea?'

I didn't know if I'd heard him right. Did he want me to make a cup of tea? Then I realized he was waiting in the doorway, one hand on the handle, his eyebrows raised, as if waiting for an answer. Suddenly the penny dropped. Oh, he was offering to make *me* a cup of tea! I couldn't believe it. Nobody had ever offered to make me anything. 'Oh, erm, yes please,' I stammered. 'That would be lovely. One sugar, thanks.'

Alan nodded towards Emily, who was now bouncing up and down on the sofa next to me. Just 15 months old, the whole thing was like one big adventure to her.

'She's the spit of you!' he said admiringly. 'She's absolutely gorgeous.'

'Oh thanks.' I was embarrassed. Nobody saw us together, certainly nobody from outside the Church, so it was strange hearing this compliment. I took her hands and led her off the sofa and down to the floor, as Alan busied himself in the kitchen. After I'd changed her nappy and dressed her in her day clothes, I took her through the hallway to the toilet. I didn't want to be apart from her for a second.

After I'd been to the loo, brushed my teeth and washed my face, I walked into the kitchen. It was a lovely sunny room with yellow walls, pine cupboards and a long refectory table with benches. I sat down on one end while Alan prepared breakfast.

'Leah had to go to work early and she took Michael into school,' he said. 'She'll join us later for dinner. How you feeling?'

'Erm, OK, I guess,' I mumbled. I felt awkward and shy around Alan all of a sudden. He had moved on with his life – I felt like an intruder.

'Please, relax Annabelle,' he tried to reassure me. 'Nobody knows you're here. Nobody is going to come looking for you. Have a bit of breakfast then we can catch up properly.'

He put a steaming mug of tea and a plate of buttered toast on the table – and handed me another plate with scrambled eggs, bacon and fried tomatoes.

'I didn't know what you wanted so I went for the works,' he smiled crookedly. Then he nodded at Emily: 'I suppose you can give her some of yours?'

I nodded enthusiastically, looking down at the feast in front of me, my nostrils filling with the wonderful, heady scent of fried bacon. All of a sudden I was ravenous. I plonked Emily next to me and fed her egg and bits of toast, as I demolished the meal. It was glorious – the taste of freedom!

Afterwards, satisfied and happy, I filled Emily's bottle with milk and, while she was drinking, I started to tell Alan a little bit about what life had been like since he left. Somehow the hours slid by and, before we knew it, it was late in the afternoon and I was still talking. I told him all about the rules – but I left out some crucial details, like all the sex stuff.

A couple of times I had to leave the room to go to the toilet and every time I got up Emily jumped up too with a panicked look on her face and put her arms out to me: 'Mama Mama Mama!'

She was desperate not to be left behind, traumatized from all the times I'd left her alone and now I had to try and make up for it.

Later on, Alan picked up his five-year-old son Michael from school and we played with him. Later still his partner Leah came home – she worked as an office administrator and was kind and warm.

'I just want to say thank you so much for having us here,' I stuttered, as we all tucked into Alan's home-made pizza that night.

'You're very welcome, Annabelle,' she replied. 'All of you. Alan's told me a little bit about the Church and how close you two were before. I know things have been really tough recently but now you're here, I'm sure things are going to be so much better.'

I hoped so too and, as I dozed off that night on the sofa again, curled protectively around Emily, some of the anxiety and fear of the past few weeks began to ease away. *It's going to be fine*, I told myself as I slid into unconsciousness. *Everything's going to be fine*.

Thomas arrived two days later and, by the sounds of it, Colin had accepted my leaving in his usual blasé manner.

'If she thinks she can get by on her own then let her go ahead and do it,' he said dismissively when Thomas relayed the news of my midnight flit.

Hope and Elaine had been a bit more upset. According to Thomas, Hope had cried and called me a 'selfish cow' for leaving. I could see why she thought I was abandoning her and, although I didn't like her to call me names, some part of me felt pleased at least that she was upset at my leaving. My mum apparently had said nothing.

I was so grateful to Thomas for everything, I kept up the charade that we were a couple. He was our saviour – he had arranged it all and now I knew I had to keep up my end of the bargain and be together as a family. Though it pained me, I allowed him to be around Emily as much as he liked. The one thing I didn't give him was sex – I was through with all that. Frankly, I never wanted to have sex again.

Of course, life on the outside wasn't at all as I imagined it. To begin with, I was scared to go out on my own. We were still only half an hour from Kidwelly, so I was petrified of bumping into Colin every time I set foot outside the house. Also, Colin's voice was still in my head. After twelve years under his control, it was all I knew.

I believed that now I had turned my back on the Gods, they had withdrawn their protection. It meant I could walk out the house and get struck down by a bus at any moment and the thought scared me. I didn't even run downstairs any more in case I fell over. And when Emily started getting a cold I was petrified Colin and the Gods had put a curse on her.

We came to an arrangement with Alan and his family – for £50 a week we rented their dining room, which we turned into a bedroom while we waited to get council accommodation. Thomas was still at work most days while I stayed in the house with Alan, who was currently between jobs. One afternoon he cracked open a bottle of Jack Daniel's and offered me some. I'd never drunk alcohol before but now, out of Colin's clutches, I was free to do whatever I liked. I could have a drink if I liked. It was up to me.

So, tentatively I took a sip. Whoah! The fiery liquid burned my throat all the way down to my stomach and my cheeks flamed instantly with the internal heat. I took a couple more glugs and before long I was opening up in a way I'd never done with anyone before.

'You're very close, you and Emily,' Alan noted. Emily was having her midday nap on the sofa next to me, and I stroked her curly dark hair.

'Not as much as I'd like,' I replied ruefully. 'I wasn't allowed to take care of her the past few months.'

'Really? Why not?'

'Colin sent me to work for the Church. Well, he says it was for the Church – I think it was actually just for him. I saw him buy loads of stuff with the money I earned him. Cars, new fur-niture, TV, clothes, holidays. Loads of nice stuff.'

'What? How did you earn enough money to buy him cars and holidays?'

'I was a prostitute,' I told him frankly. 'I earned two or three grand working three days a week. I hated it. I wanted to be with Emily, but he made the other Church members look after her and they never did it right. She always had a sore bum from sitting in a soiled nappy the whole time. I missed her first word, the first time she walked. By the end, it felt like she wasn't even my daughter any more. Everyone else seemed to know her better than me – they were all telling me what she was like. It was horrible.'

Silence.

Alan's eyes were wide and his mouth hanging open in com-plete shock.

'What? What the . . . I mean. Really? You were a *prostitute*? He made you work as a prostitute?'

'Mmmm,' I nodded, taking another swig of the Jack Daniel's. 'It was me, Mum and a few others. It was part of our path – we each had to sleep with a certain amount of men to achieve our path of becoming the Scarlet Woman. He said once we got to a certain number of people that we'd had sex with we could stop, but Mum had already got to the number and she was still doing it and I was nearly there and I knew even after I achieved the number he wouldn't let me stop.'

There was a pause. I looked over at Alan, whose head was in his hands. His eyes had filled with tears and he looked utterly distraught. Finally he asked in a cracked voice: 'What was the number you got to?'

'It was 1,800,' I said, looking him square in the eye. At that moment a sob escaped him and he shut his eyes. He began to shake then and I realized what I had told him was awful, terrible.

'I'm sorry,' I said. 'I didn't mean to upset you.'

At that moment he got up and walked over to where I was sitting on the sofa. He knelt down and enveloped me in an enormous bear hug, still crying.

'No, *I'm* sorry, Annabelle,' he whispered. 'I'm so, so sorry. I let you down. I let that monster take you and look what he did! Please forgive me.'

Then I started to cry and, for a long while, we stayed like that, me wrapped in his huge arms, crying softly. For the rest of the afternoon I told him about my secret life as a prostitute in Bristol and Alan told me again and again how wrong it was. I guess I had an idea it wasn't right from the beginning, but hearing Alan's reaction made me understand a little better that being forced into prostitution aged eighteen had been a horrendous act of betrayal.

'I guess some part of me always knew it was wrong,' I told him. 'I hated it. I hated every minute of it. But I couldn't say no. Nobody could ever say no to Colin. He controlled us all. That's why I had to get away.'

We talked like this all night until, eventually, my head spinning, my tongue thick with alcohol, I passed out on the sofa.

Come the morning I had a banging headache and I felt rough as anything. Now I knew why drinking was not a good idea! After that night of revelations, I begged Alan not to tell anyone what I'd told him, especially not Thomas or Leah. I couldn't bear for Thomas to know the truth about my 'work' for the Church and, as for Leah, I didn't want her to think less of me while I was living in her house.

Alan agreed to keep my secret. He was so good to us. All the time we were there he cooked us dinner, looked after us and accompanied me on my rare trips outside the house. Early on, I wanted to buy a buggy, so he took me to the baby shop and stood by patiently while I agonized over my decision.

Standing under the harsh neon strip-lights, I felt a rising panic as I surveyed each of the buggies in front of me. I had no idea which one to choose. All of a sudden I was in charge of my money – I had my benefits and the £3,000 I'd saved up – but I wasn't used to having choices and the responsibility of taking even the tiniest decisions made me fret like crazy. This one was impossible. Eventually Alan helped me pick one but I was still worrying about whether I'd made the right choice days later.

Even the smallest questions like: 'What do you want for dinner?' sent me into a frenzy of fussing and I'd usually end up saying 'Whatever you're having'.

But Alan would press me for an answer: 'It has to be your choice, Annabelle. You can have what you like. Think about it. What do you want?'

What do I want?

What do I want?

The question plagued me day and night – at the supermarket I couldn't make a single decision, let alone the hundreds required to get through a normal shopping trip. I'd look down at my list and the words would start to swim meaninglessly on the page.

Socks for Emily, I'd written.

Socks — what kind of socks? What colour? What size? How much should I pay? How many should I buy? Are they cheaper here? Should I even be buying cheap ones? Does she really need socks? Maybe I should buy tights? I couldn't trust my instincts because I'd never been taught to believe in them. My choices were Colin's choices — without him I was lost.

There were many trips I had to abandon halfway through, as I fled the supermarket on the verge of tears.

What did I want?

I wanted freedom, I really did. But now that I had it, it was so much harder than I'd ever imagined.

By September we'd moved into a place of our own down the road from Alan, but I was never comfortable there. Thomas still had his job in Tenby, so he was working away a lot and on my own in the flat with Emily I felt panicky and scared. Out of the flat I felt no better. I was terrified of bumping into Colin. At least I was starting to find my relations again — I had managed to find a phone number for my grandparents on the internet in the library.

It was nerve-racking making that first call, but Granddad seemed so happy to hear my voice. They were still living in London and he was thrilled to discover I was now a mother myself. Would I bring Emily to visit him and my Nan? Happy for any chance to get out of Wales, I agreed in a flash and, the next week, I was on a train down to see them. It was the first time I'd taken Emily on a train and she was so excited she couldn't sit still. Everything was new for her and, I suppose, new to me too.

The weekend with my grandparents was nice but, after so long without any contact, we were stiff and awkward around each other. When they asked about Mum I told them she was still in Kidwelly and they asked me if I'd speak to her on their behalf – they wanted to meet Moses.

'I can't really do that,' I told them. 'I'm not speaking to her any more.'

They looked shocked and pained but I couldn't go into the reasons why – I couldn't even begin to tell them what life was like with my mum. It was when my aunt Kate came over that I felt myself relax. She was so pleased to see me she threw her arms around me and then staggered back in amazement when she saw Emily peeping shyly from behind my legs.

'Oh my God!' she exclaimed with delight. 'Is that your little girl? Oh, Anna, she's beautiful! She really is! Come here, poppet, give your great aunt a cuddle then!' Emily warmed to her immediately and I was surprised that she went to her so willingly. After a couple of days, Kate invited us to stay with her.

Lying back on her sofa a few days later, I watched as Emily played with Kate and wondered if it was time to come back down south. It felt good to be near my family and far away from Colin.

'Can I take her to see the river tomorrow?'

Kate's question suddenly penetrated my thoughts.

'What?'

'She likes water, doesn't she? Well, she'd love the Thames. I could take her out to one of the bridges, give you the morning off.'

'Erm, oh, er . . .' I didn't want to say no to my aunt; I didn't want to offend her. But at the same time I never let Emily out of my sight. I was fiercely protective.

'How long for?' I asked.

'Oh, just a couple of hours,' she smiled. 'It will be nice for us two to get to know each other better.'

'OK,' I agreed, but my stomach was already in knots, full of anxiety.

'Where are they? Where are they?' I paced the room manically, asking my question over and over. It was the morning of the great river trip and I'd kissed Emily goodbye with a fake smile and a great deal of fussing. They'd been out for an hour now but it was already more than I could bear.

'What's up with you?' asked Gavin, Kate's long-term partner. I was getting more and more deranged by the minute.

'Shouldn't they be back by now?' I asked him, wringing my hands with worry. 'Where has she taken her? Do you think they'll be back soon?'

'Annabelle, Annabelle – slow down. Sit down, for God's sake, you'll wear a hole in the carpet! Look, don't worry, they'll be back soon. Let's have a cup of coffee, hmmm?'

I agreed and, as we were sipping our drinks in the lounge, Gavin distracted me by asking me about what I'd been up to the last few years.

'Oh, you know,' I replied absent-mindedly. 'This and that – school, college, work.'

'Yeah? You worked in Kidwelly?'

'No, I was working away.'

'Oh, right – as a carer or something?'

'No, as a prostitute.'

It was like I'd smacked him in the face with a frying pan: 'You what? You worked as a prostitute? Why? Did you choose to do it?'

'No, nothing like that. I was made to do it.'

And then I told Gavin all about Bristol and Colin. For some reason it felt easy to talk to him – he wasn't family, so I knew it wouldn't upset him as much as telling someone like Kate or my granddad. Still, he cried quite a bit. When Kate got back with Emily I jumped up with delight and couldn't stop grinning to have my daughter back again. Gavin's eyes meanwhile were red and puffy.

Kate gave him a quizzical look and he just shook his head in response. The next day we were due to leave and this time it was Gavin who was frantic.

'She shouldn't leave,' he told Kate firmly. 'She should stay down here and make a new life for herself in London.'

Kate seemed baffled – Gavin was genuinely very upset at our going.

'I have to go back to Thomas,' I said loyally. 'But I'll talk about it with him. Maybe we could move down here.'

As we were leaving Gavin squeezed me hard: 'Are you OK if I tell Kate? She has to understand.'

I nodded. In a way it was easier than telling her myself.

It wasn't hard to persuade Thomas to move to London. He had tired of commuting to Tenby from Carmarthen, and I knew that he too lived in fear of bumping into Colin or someone from the Church. So, two weeks before Christmas, we moved down to London and into Kate and Gavin's place. Alan was sad to see me leave, but I promised to stay in touch. When we got off the train in London I finally felt like our lives could begin afresh. Now out of Wales, I was truly free.

Chapter 19

Oblivion

'Get out!' I screamed at Thomas. 'Just leave!'

'I'm going,' he yelled back. 'I'm not sticking around here for another minute.'

'Fine. Go and don't come back!'

The door slammed shut and suddenly there was silence.

It was a month after we'd moved to London and, from the word go, there were problems between us. I'd found a job quite quickly in a clothes warehouse, but it was all the way at the other end of London. We had our own flat, but now I spent most of the week commuting to my crummy warehouse job, while Thomas was in charge of Emily.

Once again I had to leave her for hours at a time and it killed me. We told each other it was just until he found a job but, right now, that was proving difficult. Plus, he'd started to act funny.

He was calling me up all hours of the day, checking where I was, and then, on the rare occasions I met up with Kate, he was suspicious of me and one time even followed me to the super-market.

I'd turned round and got the shock of my life when I found he was just behind me, his face tucked into his grey hoodie, to stop me spotting him. For a moment I was too startled to speak, but then I got angry.

'What are you doing?' I'd demanded.

'Nothing,' he'd replied moodily. 'What are *you* doing?'

'I don't believe this!' I'd stormed. 'Go away and stop following me. It's creepy!'

Later that day, I popped into Kate and Gavin's and told them I'd started to get a funny feeling about Thomas. I don't know what it was – maybe he was going over the top trying to keep an eye on me because he'd never had any control himself. Or maybe he was just full of fear for us now that we were out of the protection of the Church. All I knew was that it was getting out of hand and I couldn't cope with it any more. I was feeling crowded and controlled and, worse, he had been in touch with Colin. He kept suggesting we go back there for a visit, just to show Colin that we were coping on our own.

It was strange – after all we'd done to try and escape I couldn't believe he was suggesting we return. I knew I had to protect the hard-won freedom I'd achieved so far so, just weeks into our new life in London, I sent him packing.

Now it was just Emily and me, I couldn't carry on working. I gave up the flat and moved in with Kate and Gavin, who were only too happy to have us. By now Kate knew all about my time in Bristol and gradually other bits of information slipped out.

One day we were talking about Thomas leaving. He'd texted me to say he was back in Kidwelly. Knowing he'd gone straight back to the Church, I felt confident that I'd done the right thing.

'He won't see her again,' I said to Kate, as we shared a glass of wine one night. By now, I'd developed quite a taste for alcohol. It numbed my feelings, gave me a sense that everything was going to be OK, even though I didn't know what I was doing from one day to the next.

'But won't he try and get access to her through the courts?' Kate asked, concerned. 'He is her dad after all.'

I shook my head: 'Nope – he's not the dad.'

'What? What do you mean? I thought you said it was him.'

'No,' I repeated. 'Not him. It's Colin. Colin's the father. He was having sex with me from when I was eleven. He made me go to bed with Thomas, too, to make it look like I was in a normal relationship. That's how he got away with it, you see. Nobody knew. Nobody knew she was really his.'

Now it was Kate's turn to look horrified.

'Colin was having sex with you from when you were a child?'

I nodded, taking another long swig of white wine.

'He abused you from when you were eleven?'

'What do you mean, "abused"?'

I'd never thought about it like this. Colin had always asked me first if I'd wanted to do the tests, so I always assumed it was my choice.

'You were a *child*, Annabelle.' Kate spoke slowly and deliberately. 'A child who was abused by a much older man. What he did to you was sick. Unforgivable.'

'He always said it was my choice, my path. But you know, I never felt like I had much choice in the matter.'

'A child can't choose to have sex,' she said. 'It was rape, Annabelle. You were raped and you should report him to the police. He shouldn't get away with it.'

Rape?

I couldn't take it in. I always thought that rape meant a stranger snatching you off the street and holding a knife to your throat and forcing you to have sex. I never imagined for a moment that what Colin did to me was rape. There was no violence, no force. It was all done because apparently I'd chosen to do it.

For days and weeks afterwards, I was in shock. I'd look at Emily and suddenly I'd see his face and then I had to look away. Was she a child of rape? My beautiful baby girl who was everything to me, my very world – she was the result of rape? It was too much. I started to go out more. There was nobody to stop me now. I could go out if I wanted, so I took to going down the local pub of an evening, first with Kate or Gavin, and later on my own.

I met a few blokes down there and one called Liam took a shine to me. With a couple of drinks inside me I became flirtatious and soon we were snogging in the middle of the pub. He took me back to his place and that night I had sex with him. I texted Kate at 11 p.m.: Met someone nice. Staying out. See you tomorrow morning.

I felt reckless and impulsive. I knew Emily would be all right because she had Kate and Gavin, and with this bloke I felt like losing myself. At around 2 a.m. he unwrapped a small white envelope.

'It's coke,' he said. 'You want some?'

I shrugged. Why not?

Within an hour I felt invincible. The coke made me feel like I could fight the world and now I showed Liam exactly what I could do. It wasn't like I even liked sex at this stage – it was just that I knew, after all those months in the brothel, I was good at it. I felt like showing off. So we took coke and screwed all night long, me acting like a porn star, driving him crazy. At 6 a.m. I tottered home still high and buzzing from the drugs. I felt rotten the next day, of course, but by then Liam had already texted to meet up again.

And so it began – my slow descent into self-destruction. I'd spent so long on a leash that, finally freed, I decided to do what the hell I liked. I didn't want to face reality any more – the real world was bloody awful. In it, I was an abused child and my daughter the product of rape. It was too much to handle. I yearned to block it all out, to lose myself in drink, drugs and sex with Liam. What did I want? I wanted oblivion. Conveniently Liam was a small-time drugs dealer, so he got all our coke for free and every weekend we met up for marathon sex and drugs parties, just the two of us locked away in his flat.

I started to neglect Emily. During the week, I was always on a comedown, feeling depressed, dirty and ashamed of myself. Now I could barely bring myself to look at Emily, let alone play with her. To cope with the depression I started taking coke during the week and, once I could block out all feelings altogether, I could act like a mother without actually being one.

It was Kate and Gavin who saved me. One day, a couple of months after I started seeing Liam, they found my coke stash and went ballistic. They threw me out of the house with a warning: get clean or risk losing Emily altogether.

It was the wake-up call I needed. I went to stay with my Aunt Becca and stopped the coke immediately. Suddenly all the emotions I'd held back for so long came pouring out of me and, lying in the spare bed in Becca's flat, I wept for three days solid.

'I can't lose her, Becca,' I sobbed. 'I can't lose Emily. She's everything to me. She's my world but I've hurt her again, Becca. I've let her down again. I'm a terrible mum.'

'Shhhh,' she soothed, her arms around me. 'You're not a terrible mum at all. You've just been through a rough patch. It's going to be fine. Just focus on her now and getting yourself well again.'

Straight away I broke up with Liam. He didn't know where I lived, so there was no chance of him coming to find me. This meant I went cold turkey with the coke. It was hard at first – my emotions were everywhere – but within a couple of weeks I was getting back to myself again. I'd been visiting Emily every day now, and when I sat down to talk to Kate she saw how genuine and upset I was at being separated from my daughter.

'I'm clean,' I told her. 'I know I came off the rails for a while there but I'm back again. Can I please come back? I don't know if I can go on any longer without her.'

Kate looked at Gavin and he nodded and then she said, 'Yes. Yes, of course you can come back. She needs you, Annabelle. She needs her mum.'

And with that I collapsed sobbing into her arms. She held me for a while, then she pulled back and looked at me hard.

'You've lost a lot of weight, you know,' she said. 'You've got to get healthy again. Put some weight on.'

I nodded. I'd do anything she said.

But it wasn't all that easy. Even when I was back in Kate and Gavin's flat, I found it difficult to put on weight. I knew my arms and legs were now looking very slim, sticklike even. Kate said she was worried about me and urged me to register with a doctor, so I could get myself properly checked out.

'I'm sure everything is fine,' she said practically. 'I'm sure it's just the stresses and strains of everything you've been through the past year, but it's probably best to get a check-up. You know – just to be on the safe side.'

I knew what she was thinking – all that time in the brothel sleeping with strangers. And now it seemed I was losing weight rapidly. Had I caught something sinister?

'I don't want to do it,' I told her. It was hard enough living with all the truths I'd uncovered since coming out of Kidwelly. It was hard enough facing up to my past. Now I had to potentially face a life-threatening illness?

'If there is something wrong, if there is,' she said, 'then the earlier you find out, the better chance you have. You owe this to Emily. You know you do.'

I sighed. She was right.

So, a week later, on a grey, overcast day in May, I registered with a GP at a local surgery. It was the nurse I saw first. I told her my background and, when I asked for a HIV test, she took it in her stride. She took me through a number of questions and when she asked me how many people I'd slept with in the past few years I replied honestly: 'Multiple. A lot.'

'More than twenty?'

'Yes, a lot more than twenty.'

'Did you always use a barrier contraception?'

'Not always, no.' I hung my head in shame. I couldn't look her in the eye.

'OK, well, it's a simple and quick test,' she said professionally. 'Don't worry. We'll have it done here and you can have the result in half an hour. You can wait in the smaller waiting room if you wish.'

It was the longest half an hour of my life and, when my name was finally called, my heart was pounding like crazy. I must have looked petrified because as soon as the nurse showed me into the room she smiled and said: 'Relax, it's negative.'

I breathed out with relief: 'Oh, thank you. Thank you so much.'

'That's OK. We can go through your results in more detail, if you like, but just to give you an overview, it looks like you are clear of all sexually transmitted and non-sexually transmitted infections including gonorrhoea, chlamydia, herpes, syphilis, hepatitis and, of course, HIV.'

I was so relieved I could barely speak.

'Are you OK?' she asked me.

'Yeah, yes, I'm fine, thank you,' I finally replied, smiling and blinking in amazement.

There was a pause and the nurse looked at me with real

concern. 'You've been very lucky, you know. You were in the high-risk category.'

That wiped the smile off my face.

Her words were still echoing round my head as I re-emerged into the daylight on that dull and cloudy day. Pulling my thin denim jacket around me, I heard the nurse's voice again: 'You were very lucky.'

Why did that bother me so much? Why didn't I feel happy, elated even, that I was all clear from infection? I started walking back towards the tube to go home to Kate and Gavin, who were minding Emily.

Very lucky. I heard her words again, as my boots clipped the pavement. She said I was lucky. A lucky escape. Lucky.

And then it struck me. I *was* lucky. I was lucky because I was out of there! But Moses and Olivia were still there. What if they weren't so lucky? What if Colin made them do things and they got ill? I stopped still and took my phone out of my bag.

Instinctively I dialled Kate and Gavin's home number.

Gavin picked up: 'Annabelle, are you OK? Is everything OK?'

'Yes, I'm fine,' I replied. 'Everything's clear.'

'Oh, thank God for that! Oh, we're so pleased for you sweetheart . . .'

'Listen, Gavin,' I stopped him mid-sentence. 'I want to go to the police. I want to report Colin to the police.'

There was a momentary pause then Gavin replied, 'Where are you? I'll pick you up and take you there now.'

Chapter 20

Facing Up to the Past

It was time to face up to my past, for the sake of the ones I had left behind. So on that day in May, Gavin picked me up from outside the doctor's surgery and took me straight round to the local police station.

'No point waiting around for you to change your mind,' he said as he drove. 'Might as well strike while the iron is hot.'

I felt slightly dazed and nervous as I walked into a police station for the first time. I had no idea what to do, so I let Gavin take control. He spoke to the sergeant behind the desk.

'Her name is Annabelle Forest and she's here to make a statement,' he explained. 'It's about a lot of things – she was in a cult, this is about child abuse and rape and prostitution. There are a number of people involved.'

The police told us they would have to make the necessary arrangements for a formal video interview and asked us to return the next morning. At that point I didn't think anybody would take me seriously but gradually events would start to gather momentum and the whole thing would snowball out of control.

'Are you OK, Annabelle?' asked the kind policewoman on the other side of the table. Of course I was really scared, but I tried to stay calm. I nodded and she signalled to her colleague to start filming. I'd reported to the police station with Gavin the next morning as they'd asked, and now we were all set. One of the policewomen asked the questions, the other one wrote down my answers, and Gavin sat nearby, for moral support. By the end of the first day I was exhausted and upset but we had barely scratched the surface.

On day two there were more police officers in the room with us, but I tried to concentrate on the policewoman questioning me. When we got to the bits about having to have sex with Colin and my mum, I looked over to see some of the police officers wiping away tears. On day three when I described working in the brothel and leaving Emily, three more officers were crying. Eventually, at the end of that day's taping, the police officer said she thought they had enough for now.

'What happens next?' I asked them.

'We send your statement through to our colleagues in Wales and they make the necessary arrests based on your evidence of alleged criminal offences.'

'What criminal offences do you mean?' I asked. I was still so in the dark as to what Colin and the others had actually done to me.

'Well, first of all there's the rape, then the indecent assault, causing a child to have sex, and then causing prostitution for personal gain. And we're talking multiple offences of each.'

'Is it really rape?' I still couldn't get my head around this idea. 'I mean, Colin never forced me to do anything. He never spoke words that were nasty or abusive. It wasn't like that. He always told me I was special. It was always flattering and then he would ask me if I agreed to a test and I'd say yes and that was it.'

'But you were a child – you didn't understand what you were saying yes to,' the policewoman explained patiently.

'That's true.'

'A child can't give their consent to sex, because they don't know what it is. They are incapable of making such a choice, therefore it is rape. It doesn't have to be forced or violent for it to be rape. Around ninety per cent of rape cases are committed by a person known to the victim. It's more common than a case of a stranger snatching someone randomly off the street.'

'I knew it wasn't right what happened to me, but at the time it seemed normal.'

'Frightening, isn't it?' reflected the policewoman. 'How quickly a child can get used to a horrific state of affairs.'

Then the policewoman asked me whether I thought my own daughter had been abused and it was this question I'd been hiding from for so long. I didn't want to think about it.

Distraught and guilty, I told her: 'I don't know. I don't think so, but I honestly don't know. I wasn't there.'

And suddenly the helplessness I'd felt during all those months when I was sent away from her, the pain of hearing her gut-wrenching screams as I walked out the door, came bubbling to the surface and tears sprung to my eyes.

'I really hope not because . . .' I could barely get my words out I was sobbing so hard. 'I'd never forgive myself if he did.'

For a while I cried and the policewoman sat patiently waiting for me to finish. She handed me a tissue and then, quietly, she said:

'Annabelle – there is a way of finding out.'

I looked up warily.

'Yeah, it's um . . . it's not very nice for her,' the policewoman admitted.

'A physical examination?' I asked.

'Mmm,' she nodded.

'Would it hurt her?'

'I'm not going to lie to you – it's quite an ordeal.'

That made my mind up. I'd already put my daughter through enough during the past two years. I couldn't bear to inflict any more pain on her.

'No,' I told her firmly. 'No, I don't think anything happened to her and I don't think there's any point doing a test that's going to be traumatic for her, so let's just leave it.'

'Fair enough,' she replied. 'Well, if you ever change your mind . . .'

I shook my head, pushing the thought away.

'No, I won't. Nothing happened to her and that's that.'

From the last day of my statement, things moved at a startling pace. The police called the following day – they had arrested my mum and Colin. All of a sudden I felt a wave of regret and pity. I couldn't help it – she was still my mum and I cared about her. Colin had been the most important person in my life until just a year ago. They had just been sitting in the kitchen, having a cup of tea, minding their own business when suddenly their lives were turned upside down.

Now there were consequences and, for the first time, I began to appreciate just what I had done. Moses and Olivia were taken into temporary foster care, as my mum and Colin were held on remand. Word quickly came back – they were both denying everything. Oh, God, I worried late at night, what have I done? What's going to happen next?

A week later, two Welsh policewomen came down to London and I did some more interviews. They had found certain things in my mum and Colin's houses and wanted to know what they were. They showed me videos they'd found – one of me at fifteen. I'd forgotten all about this. Colin recorded a video of me standing at the end of the bed – first he made me lift my skirt up, then he pulled my top up. I felt sickened and ashamed as I watched my shy and embarrassed 15-year-old self expose herself to the camera on Colin's commands.

'We just need you to confirm, Annabelle, if that's you or not,' the Welsh policewoman said kindly.

But I felt anger building inside me.

'Of course it's me,' I hissed. 'You can see that for yourself. Do I have to watch any more of this?'

I couldn't bear to see her – that innocent, trusting girl of fifteen who did as she was told without a murmur of dissent. I felt pity for her, yes, but at the same time I hated her for obeying his every command, for allowing herself to be manipulated like this.

'It wasn't your fault!' Kate insisted later that night, when I told her about the video and the feeling I had when I watched it, being disgusted with myself.

'You were a child! None of this was your fault.'

'How did he have so much power over our lives?' I fumed. 'That's what I'd like to know. We'd only been there a short while and then suddenly he was in charge of everything! Mum just gave him all the power. You know what . . . I accept that it wasn't my fault. You can make a kid do anything. That's what I've realized. If you get a child young enough you can make them believe anything you like and then they'll do anything you want. But her? She wasn't a child! She was twenty-eight. How come she did all that stuff for him?'

'Love?' Kate ventured.

'Funny kind of love,' I shot back. 'No. No, that's not love. That's something else, that is. I just don't know what.'

For the first time in my life I was examining everything that had been done to me over the years and weighing up the people in my life and what parts they had all played. Now that I knew they were criminal acts, I started to see things more clearly. But with that clarity also came a huge surge of anger. Every day I woke up angrier and more determined to see Colin and my mum pay for what they did to me.

There were times I was so furious I didn't know what to do with myself – I'd just sit still, boiling with rage, frightened that if I got up or moved around I'd do something dangerous. The police offered me counselling but I only lasted one session. I couldn't even begin to address my feelings about the past until I'd put my abusers behind bars. More than anything, what I needed was justice. I needed the world to hear my voice, to hear my side of things and to know the pain and anger I felt. It felt stupid and pointless talking to a woman in a large cardigan about it.

Over the following months, more witnesses came forward; one girl I'd never even heard of before claimed the abuse went back years. I should have felt grateful for their support but it only fuelled my rage. Where had they been all these years? Why did they leave Kidwelly without telling the police? Their silence had condemned me to a childhood of horrific abuse.

Elaine, Shelley and Sandra were arrested. Now the police were calling me up every week with further questions and I began to shrink back into myself with fear. Every time I opened my mouth someone else was arrested, so I became frightened to tell them anything. It was only my mum and Colin who had done stuff to me. I didn't hold anything against the others – as far as I could see, most of them were victims of Colin too, and I didn't want to get any more people into trouble.

At night I confided my fear and confusion to Kate.

'You've been so incredibly brave, Annabelle,' she said. 'I know none of this can be easy but you're doing the right thing.'

'How do you know?' I demanded. 'How can any of us know? I don't know if Moses being in foster care is any better for him than being at home with mum. And what if innocent people go to jail?'

'They won't,' she insisted.

'No, you *think* they won't, but you don't know for certain,' I countered. 'Now it's out of our hands and who's to say where it will all end? It feels like the repercussions are just getting bigger and bigger and it's too much for me. That's *my* sister, *my* brother, in foster care and I put them there! How do you think that makes me feel?'

'I don't know, Annabelle,' she replied quietly. 'How does it feel?'

'Bloody awful. It feels bloody awful.'

Next, I got death threats on my mobile phone from one of the Church members. I reported it to the police straight away and the person was arrested but even this swift action didn't reassure me.

Even though I was hundreds of miles away from Kidwelly, I was always looking over my shoulder. Now my nights were plagued by nightmares too. One was particularly vivid, of me sitting in my kitchen in Kidwelly and Colin walking in the back door covered with blood.

When I told Kate about it, she said it sounded like I felt guilty about Colin. And perhaps she was right – I was destroying him now and I did feel guilty about it.

'*You're* not destroying him,' Kate insisted. 'He did it all himself. He was the one who raped and abused little girls. You didn't make him do that. You're the one who's stopping him from doing it again.'

I sat back then and sighed: 'You know, for ages I thought it was about something more, that our religion was really important and that we were all trying to reach a higher spiritual plane. I believed him. We all did. But, the more I think about it, the more I think it was all just to satisfy Colin and his appetites for sex and money. It's disappointing. Can you understand that? I really thought he could show us something better, a path to a beautiful place. Even now I wonder if he still believes it all. He's been the person I've listened to all my life. He brought me up, he was everything to me. It's really hard. It's like chopping off your own arm.'

Kate remained thin-lipped: 'He made you keep his dirty little secrets for too long, Annabelle. He's got into your head.'

'I know that!' I fumed. 'He's always there, whether I like it or not. They can lock him up on the outside, but they can't take him out of my skull!'

That year was as tough as anything, but I did a lot of thinking and growing up in that time. Every day I'd hear something new from the police. The other girls were refusing to give evidence against Colin; they said they had chosen to work in the brothel themselves. It killed me, but I knew they were brainwashed, the same as I had been for all that time. Finally, the trial date was set for February 2011 at Swansea Crown Court, nine months after I first went to the police. Colin, Elaine, Mum and the others were all pleading not guilty. According to the police Colin had denied all the charges, calling them 'a load of rubbish'.

He had even denied that he was a follower of Crowley's *The Book of The Law*. I was gobsmacked when the police said he'd told them he had tried reading it but gave up and was actually a Mormon who followed the Bible.

Gavin drove me up to Swansea the night before I was due to give evidence. As we headed up the M4, out of London and back towards Wales for the first time since my escape, I felt my fingers balling into fists at my side. I wasn't scared any more. I was determined. The time had finally come to tell the world what Colin had done. It was time to lift the lid on all those years of Church secrecy.

Chapter 21

The Trial

In the end I gave my evidence via video link from another room, so I didn't see Colin, my mum, Elaine or any of the others. Even so, I found every single second on the stand excruciating. It was like my worst nightmare come true: the idea that all these people in the court, including my mum and Colin, could see me, but I couldn't see them, was scary. And I had to reveal to these faceless people the most sordid, unpleasant aspects of my childhood. It felt like I was standing there naked, all my most awful secrets laid bare to the world.

While I gave my evidence for the prosecution, the camera pointed to the judge, so I talked to him, trying to put aside the thought of all the other people in the room, trying desperately to hide my shame and embarrassment. Then, as the defence lawyers started questioning me, the camera turned to face them in turn. Not once did it show the defendants, though, which was something I was grateful for.

At first some of the questions seemed straightforward but, gradually, I realized they were intended to make me look like I was either stupid or incapable of knowing what actually happened. Mum's lawyer asked me which classes I had been in in school, knowing very well I had been put into all the low sets because I struggled academically.

It made me furious and frustrated. I wanted to shout at my mum – *why are you denying it? You know it happened. You know I'm not a liar!*

After everything that had happened I just wanted her to take responsibility for her actions. At the very least she owed me that. But no, she denied all the counts against her. I don't know what was harder, the abuse or the fact that she lied about it to the whole world, pretending I was making it all up. In the end, it was the judge who stopped the line of questioning, saying that it was going nowhere and unless there were any other questions he should sit down.

I was on the stand for two days, after which I staggered off, exhausted and angry. Because all of them were all being tried together, I had to answer questions from four different defence lawyers, and they each chose to grill me about different things. It was all so confusing and annoying.

On the walk back to our hotel in Swansea that afternoon, I found I couldn't remember a word of what I'd said or what anyone had said to me. The whole thing had been so traumatic. Gavin and I ate in silence then each went back to our rooms. Emily was in London being looked after by Kate. I was tired and flopped onto the bed, expecting to fall asleep pretty quickly but, as the minutes ticked by, the silence became oppressive. My eyes flickered open, and the depressing little room seemed to get smaller and smaller by the minute. If only Emily were here, I'd give her a massive hug right now. I got up, anxious and jittery and went across the hallway where I knocked on Gavin's door.

'Can I watch TV in your room?' I asked, when he opened up. 'I don't want to be on my own right now.'

It came out in court that the police had done a DNA test on Emily, proving once and for all that she was Colin's child. Moses too. Apparently Elaine, Colin's wife, had no idea – she learned all of this during the trial, which must have been quite a shock. In fact, everything about the case was shocking. I was only in Swansea for two days to give my evidence, but I read about the rest of the trial in the papers over the following few days. One girl said she had been initiated into the Church through sex with Colin when she was fifteen and then passed around other members like a sex toy.

A man said Colin had tricked him into having sex with Elaine. Like myself, the courts gave them lifelong anonymity, so their identities were kept out of the papers, but I had a fair idea of who they were. Suddenly the lid was coming off all of Colin's Church secrets and there was nothing he could do to stop it. We were finally being heard and, the more people that came forward to give evidence, the more I believed that they probably wouldn't get off.

Colin gave his evidence over three days – every word of it a lie. He denied everything, only admitting to having had sex with me twice. He had to admit to it at least once because he was Emily's dad! That was proved beyond doubt – but he denied absolutely everything else, even knowing about *The Book of The Law*. I was astounded.

Prosecutor Peter Murphy talked about Aleister Crowley's *Book of The Law* and how Colin had used it to preach, quoting parts that seemed to promote rape and prostitution. One part he read out loud:

'Some of the most passionate and permanent attachments have begun with rape. Rome was founded thereon.'

When Mr Murphy asked Colin about it, he said: 'Rape is wrong.'

Mr Murphy replied: 'But that doesn't appear to be what the book is saying, does it?'

Colin said: 'No, it doesn't.'

Another section the jury heard was: 'Let all chaste women be utterly despised.' And then: 'Sex with anyone is not just permissible but to be encouraged. Prostitution is to be admired.'

Mr Murphy said: 'Is that a clue about how you saw things? Was that your world, a world you used to control and subdue children and young adults?'

Colin replied: 'No.'

I seethed when I read that bit in the papers. During the year I was on a quest to become his Scarlet Woman he had forced me to sleep with hundreds of men, all because of the writings in *The Book of The Law*. Now he was denying even knowing about it!

Later on, Mr Murphy said that during the time I worked for him as a prostitute, I would have earned Colin over £45,000.

He then asked Colin where the money was. I nearly choked when I read his reply: 'Nothing was paid to me.'

I had handed over thousands of pounds in cash, every week! All of us who had worked in the brothels were caught on CCTV, driving up and down the motorway, so there was no way any of us could deny what was happening. It's just the others said they chose to work as prostitutes.

When the prosecution asked Colin how he managed to pay a cash deposit of over £3,000 on a £21,000 caravan, despite having no obvious source of income, Colin claimed he earned up to £10,000 a year from breeding pedigree Rottweilers and Siamese cats. He also claimed he'd won money gambling on the dogs and horses. I suppose I shouldn't have been surprised. Colin had spent his whole life lying – why stop now? I just hoped that the jury would see through his deceit.

It was Elaine who surprised everyone. Apparently she had been planning to leave Colin for a while before they all got arrested and, as the revelations came out and her life collapsed around her, she began to realize that Colin was not the man she thought he was.

In the witness stand she said: 'I feel embarrassed to be married to him.' And she added: 'I've changed. You won't get the better of me now.'

As the case went on, I learned more about the sordid lives of the adults who had brought me up. Elaine admitted in court that she and my mum had been involved in 'threesomes', and that they'd even enjoyed a lesbian fling together. But she only found out later that Colin and Mum had been having a long-term affair. Apparently she made the discovery when Mum sent him a birthday card with the words 'To my husband' on it. It rang a bell when I read that part. I remember something about a card years back, when Elaine was angry with my mum. But she claimed in court she had no idea he was abusing me.

In my heart, I knew that Elaine was probably a victim of Colin too, and I did feel sorry for her in some respects. But hearing what she did to the others and how she had allowed Colin free rein confirmed that she too had crossed the line. In accepting his twisted ideas, she had also become something terrible. The woman who I'd looked up to, and even loved as a child, I was seeing for the first time as a rotten abuser, just like my mum.

My mum wasn't on the stand long, and I didn't even see any coverage of what she said in court, which was frustrating. I wanted to hear something from her, even if it was just to put all the blame on Colin. At that point I still couldn't make sense of it. More than anything in the world I needed to understand; I needed her to explain how she could go from a normal mother, like she was in London, to a woman who abused her own children and forced her to take part in group sex. How did she become that person? I really wanted to know.

But she simply denied all the charges. It was like she was telling the world that I was just lying, making it all up. I didn't expect her to admit it all and say sorry – I didn't expect that and I don't think I would have accepted an apology anyway. But I did want to know how it happened. I wanted an explanation. She was a fully grown woman with a loving family, a life, and a mind of her own. How had she allowed Colin to warp her thoughts so badly?

I was at home in London on 9 March when the police rang

through with the verdict. Guilty. Colin was found guilty of thirty-five separate offences, including eleven rapes, causing prostitution and indecency with children. Mum was found guilty of five offences, including aiding and abetting rape, causing prostitution and indecency with children. Elaine was found guilty of five counts of indecency with children and Shelley was convicted of two. Only Sandra got off.

That evening, sat in the lounge with Kate, Gavin and a celebratory glass of champagne, I wondered why I felt so empty. I wanted to feel happy and relieved, just like I'd expected I would. But no, there was nothing. No sense of satisfaction or vindication, just hollowness. Living it and then telling it to others, it was all so awful, and now these people would go to prison for their crimes.

That's what the judge said – he said they could expect lengthy prison sentences. I didn't feel glad. It was miserable. The Church world I'd been brought up in was a miserable lie to satisfy the urges of a sick and manipulative paedophile. That was the real truth of the matter. Out in the open I had seen how sordid and disgusting it had all been.

The depressing part was accepting how I'd been fooled for all those years. How I'd been manipulated into thinking there was something more to it than just sex. I'd lived and breathed Colin, the Church and his words for so many years, it was painful to let it all go. I needed one more thing. One more chance to find out the truth from mum. I asked Gavin that night: 'Will you take me to the sentencing? I have to see her. I have to look in her eyes.'

* * *

We left the house at 5 a.m. the following day to take the train to Swansea to hear the sentencing. Once again, Kate stayed in London to look after Emily, so Becca came with us. For the first time I walked into the courtroom where my mum and her lovers, Colin, Elaine and Shelley, had been tried. I looked around me – there was activity everywhere. Reporters jostled for space among uniformed officers, black-gowned lawyers and a large group of family members.

I tried not to look too hard – Thomas was there somewhere and he'd given evidence for the defence. I suppose I couldn't blame him – he had never known the truth. Hope, too, gave evidence for the other side. I didn't want to catch anyone's eye.

'Are you OK?' Becca whispered, as we took our seats in the public gallery. She gripped my hand in hers. I knew I was shaking from head to toe but I couldn't stop. I was about to see my mum for the first time in two years and inside I was a tangle of conflicting emotions. I wanted so much for her to turn against Colin, even at this late hour. I wanted her to show me that she cared. This was her very last chance.

Elaine came out first. Her body language said it all – her head and eyes were downcast, her shoulders slumped and she shuffled pitifully to her seat. She looked defeated. In some ways I felt sorry for Elaine. She had been in Colin's clutches since she was a teenager and believed in him more than any of us. In this court, all of that had come crashing down – he was no more than a vile paedophile and, what's more, he'd had two children behind her back. Whatever story he'd made her believe before, she no longer believed it now. Shelley came up next – she looked the same as always. Head up, chin jutting out, arrogant as usual. She threw disdainful looks about her as she sat down.

And then came my mum. At first I almost didn't recognize her. It had been two years since I'd last seen her but, even so, her changed appearance was shocking. Now she was thin and fragile with long and straggly grey hair, like an old woman. I gasped when I realized it was her. She seemed so frail and delicate. I wondered in that moment if she would survive prison. Finally Colin came up. By contrast he had filled out during the year he had been held on remand. Normally skinny as a rake, he now sported an unpleasant belly and his face was puffy and bloated. He sat next to Mum and smiled at her. That awful crooked smile with the single tooth.

Strangely, I didn't feel anything when I saw Colin. I didn't hate him. I felt nothing for him. The only one I cared about was my mum. Seeing the way she smiled back at him, at the affection she clearly held for him, I felt so angry I wanted to run down there, grab and shake her. I wanted to scream in her face: *'What are you doing? Why are you protecting him? It's over. Even if it's not about me, why choose him over Moses? Why do you want to go to prison for Colin? Why choose him over your own children?'*

But of course I didn't move or say a word. I was rooted to the spot, unable to even catch my breath. Then I saw mum scanning the public gallery and her eyes caught mine. My heart thumped wildly in my chest: Mum! I wanted to call out, to reach out to her. But then she sneered at Colin, loud enough for me to hear: 'Oh, look who's here!'

It was the end. In those stark few words my mother finally

killed whatever feeling I had left for her. I knew then with complete certainty that my mother was an evil person. It wasn't just Colin. She had done those things because she wanted to. It was in her all along – meeting Colin simply brought it to the surface. Well, now I knew it in my heart and, however much it hurt to let her go, I knew for the sake of my health and sanity that I had no choice. I looked away and discreetly wiped a tear from my cheek.

Becca didn't need to say a word – she squeezed my arm and I could feel the warmth and strength flowing out of her.

It's OK – she was saying – *I'm here for you. Stay strong.*

'All rise please for his Honour Judge Paul Thomas QC.'

The next moment we were all on our feet as the judge came into court for the sentencing. There was silence as he began his report. Reporters scribbled furiously in notebooks. I was on the edge of my seat. For Colin, twenty-two years with a recommendation that he spend at least eleven in jail.

'You may never be released,' the judge told him. 'You set yourself up as ruler in your own sick little kingdom, where three women danced as your willing attendants. You became their master and formed a community within a community, involving child abuse, rape and prostitution. You have been described as evil. That, in my view, is an entirely accurate statement of your character. It is clear that you have dedicated your life since you were twelve years old to satisfying your sexual urges by whatever means at your disposal. The age or sex of your victims was largely a matter of indifference to you.

'You treated one victim as nothing more than a sexual

plaything, dominating and controlling her life, and you persuaded your wife to join in. What happened has besmirched the unsuspecting town of Kidwelly.'

He added: 'You are, and for the foreseeable future, a danger to children. This has been your life's work, involving multiple offences over many years. The public needs protection from you; there are very serious concerns and risks in the future if you are released.'

He went on: 'You have fully lived up to the ideals of your mentor, Aleister Crowley. You used the occult to further your sexual excesses – children were kept as toys for sex purposes. You took a cruel delight in initiating children into sex but their lives have been blighted forever. It was organized and systematic abuse of children and you dedicated yourself to such depravity.'

He then addressed my mum: 'You were clearly besotted with him and this *Book of The Law*, and I view you effectively as his second-in-command.'

I was surprised when he handed her a sentence of twelve years. I was expecting her to get more. Her crimes deserved more – she'd already served a year. She would get out in five years. Five years! If someone burgled a shop they would get longer. It was less than half the time I had served under Colin. I thought of all the occasions I was forced to have sex with her and him. I grieved for my stolen childhood. *She should have got more.*

The judge read out the rest of the sentences. He said Elaine had become a willing participant in Colin's wickedness and jailed her for eight years. Shelley had been behind the prostitution side of the operation and got five years.

Driving back that evening, I felt sad knowing that even if my mum got out tomorrow our relationship was at an end. At least I had closure now. I knew there was no going back. As far as I was concerned she could spend the rest of her life in jail for the things she did. And it still wouldn't be enough. Because no matter how many years she was locked up, nothing could change my past. Nothing could bring back my childhood. The only thing I could do now was ensure Emily and I enjoyed a wonderful future. I vowed that night that I wouldn't let Mum destroy that.

Chapter 22

Grief

After the sentencing, reality hit me hard. I now knew that my mum chose to do what she did. She wasn't under Colin's spell – she knew all along what she was doing. And she knew how wrong it was. Now I had to face the rest of my life without a mother. For a long time I didn't feel safe or anchored. I'd walk down the street and see young girls with their mums and my heart would ache with envy. I wanted to be like them – I wanted a mum to turn to, to be there for me, to love. Or simply to go shopping with. It drove me crazy if I heard young kids being cheeky or rude to their parents. I'd want to give them a shake and tell them to appreciate their parents. Not everyone has good parents and those that do rarely realize it.

By now, Emily had started school and I decided to go back to college. I needed to build a positive future for us both. But I struggled in the months after the court case to maintain a positive outlook. I was grieving for my mother and for the childhood I had lost in Wales. All those emotions I'd put on hold during the court case now bubbled to the surface and I would find myself being overwhelmed in the strangest places. I could be standing in the middle of the supermarket and suddenly I would feel lost and paranoid. Why was everyone staring at me? I'd wonder. Right then, I'd want to just run back home and hide under the covers. I felt more alone than ever before.

In the midst of all this turmoil, I faced another fight. Social Services took in Moses when my mother and Colin were arrested. Now that they were behind bars for years, there was no one to look after him, so it was decided that he should be permanently fostered. At that point I knew what I had to do – I asked Social Services if they would consider me as a candidate for fostering and possible adoption. After all, he was my half-brother, and Emily's relative too. But more than that, he was the little boy I had raised from a baby.

Even though it had now been two years since I'd seen him, I still looked on him as a son. I wanted so much to do right by him, since I was responsible for the fact that he was now in foster care. He was the innocent one in all of this. Two years before, he had lost me; a year later he had lost his mum and dad on the same day. I didn't want him to grow up feeling abandoned by everyone he had known in his life. It simply wasn't fair.

Social Services came to assess me a few months after the trial. They seemed not to know much about what had happened with Colin and my mum. They didn't even know I had been the main prosecution witness in the case. While I was telling them about it all, suddenly the emotions came to the surface and I started to cry. I couldn't help it – it was like the floodgates had opened and I was only now processing what had happened to me.

The two women were very kind and understanding and I thought it had gone well. But then I got a letter three weeks later telling me that I was too emotionally unstable to care for Moses. Reading that letter made me want to scream. What did they expect? They had grilled me about the abuse I had suffered as a child. Wasn't it natural to get emotional about that? Was I supposed to be a machine?

It was so unfair. How come I was a good enough mother for Emily but not good enough for Moses? He belonged with me; I was his family. I had raised him from a baby! How dare these people take away the one member of family he had left? I ranted and raved at Kate later that day.

'Look at this!' I fumed. 'Look! It says I can send him two cards a year: one for his birthday and one for Christmas! Can you imagine? Two cards! What good is that going to do him? He won't even remember who I am in a year's time. I left him when he was four and next year he'll be seven!'

That night I sobbed and sobbed. I felt like I had let him down, that I had failed him. During this time I had also come to a decision about my granddad – the man I had loved so dearly as a child. I decided to cut him out of my life. I suppose it wasn't something that happened dramatically – it was just that, as the court case progressed, he chose to visit my mum in jail and he still spoke well of her when I was there. After she was found guilty, he carried on visiting her.

In some ways I could understand his actions – as a mother, I would find it very difficult to let go of all attachment and affection to my child if I'd known they'd done something awful. But as the innocent victim of her crimes I found his decision to take her side perverse. And hurtful. It got to a point where I could no longer stand to be in his house. I didn't even like to see him playing with Emily. Whose side was he on? Certainly not mine, certainly not Emily's.

No – in the end it became too hard to visit him when I knew that he was choosing to maintain contact with my mum. I could see it in his eyes, the way he looked at me, as if he blamed me for putting him through hell. By now Nan was suffering from Alzheimer's – and I suppose, in some ways, that was merciful. She never got to find out what her daughter did.

So now I felt very alone and very vulnerable in the world. It was as if somebody had stripped away a layer of skin and I was exposed as never before. I felt I had lost all the protection I believed I'd had when I lived in the Church. Back then, Colin had answers for all the questions in the world – what did I have to replace him with? Nothing. I didn't believe in any God or religion. So it wasn't always easy to block out Colin's voice from my head. He was always there, reminding me of how I had strayed from my path and, as a result, I was cursed, doomed to suffer a lifetime of pain.

In the back of my mind now I was constantly worried there was some kind of bad aura around me. Whatever I touched and wherever I went, there was trouble. First my Aunt Becca and Uncle Alex split up after twenty-seven years together. Then, after the court case, Kate and Gavin split up. I blamed myself.

Other things happened and I thought Colin and the Gods were punishing me. Putting him behind bars was one thing, but the brainwashing had gone on for so long that it was hard to get rid of it entirely. When I heard about bad things happening, like natural disasters or explosions, I always thought Colin was behind them somehow. He had convinced me of this awesome power he had and I guess my brain was programmed to believe this, even when I knew for a fact it wasn't true. Colin had been everything to me. He had shaped my whole identity from a young age and now I hardly knew who I was any more.

Looking back, I see how our relationship had gone through various stages – first he had been like a father figure to me, then a preacher, leader, abuser, partner and finally, boss. When I first moved next door to him he was like my father. He would tell me what to do, laying down the rules and discipline. Then he became the leader and preacher of the Church, with all the ceremonies, the readings and meetings. Then the sex thing started and I was scared of him – he was my abuser. After I had Emily he was more like a partner. Finally he moved on to become my boss and I was his sex slave.

He thought he would have power over me forever because, in so many ways, he had made me, moulded me and created the 'perfect little whore' he had always wanted. He thought I would never leave him. But he made one terrible mistake – he made me a mother. When he did that he sowed the seeds of his own destruction. Loving Emily had broken his spell. That was his one mistake. Otherwise, the abuse might have gone on for many more years.

There are some things he said so many times, I found I couldn't get them out of my head and which haunt me even today. He always used to laugh at the fact that I was flat-chested. He took the piss out of me for it. It made me very self-conscious and I would envy girls who filled out their tops. It crossed my mind over and over again that if I got a boob job, if I was only a little bit bigger, than I would be happy. And from time to time this horrid little thought bubbles to the top of my head and I curse my modest A-cup breasts. Of course, in my heart I know my breasts aren't the problem. I know that my body is perfectly nice and that my insecurities were created by the monster that raised me. But insecurities they still are, and on days I'm feeling down they can overwhelm me.

Generally, during the day, I did my best not to think about Colin – I didn't want to waste one more second of my life on him and his mind games. But then he'd find another way to infiltrate my life – through my dreams. The strangest thing of all was that they weren't all nightmares. I had one recurring dream that he was caring for Emily and me, that he was telling us: 'This is how it was always meant to be. The three of us together.' And I found some comfort in that dream – the familiarity of it, the security of it, knowing that Colin was there to protect us and take care of our futures.

Of course, I'd wake up and know for a fact that he had never protected us, that he had spent my lifetime harming me. But, without anything secure in my life afterwards, I suppose my subconscious clung to the things I knew from the past. I wanted to believe I was the 'chosen one'. I wanted to believe that some things in life were meant to be.

Then there were the nightmares. Some were so realistic they would come back in flashes during the day and I'd wonder if they had actually happened. One particularly horrible dream stayed with me for weeks. In it, Colin climbed in through my bedroom window while I was asleep, put his hand over my mouth to stop me screaming, then injected me with some kind of poison. It was all the worse for the fact that it felt so vivid, as if I really was waking up in the middle of a violent attack.

I'd feel his strong arms around me, pinning me down and I'd be lying on my bed, terrified, unable to move. Then I'd see this giant needle appear and its long tip would glint in the moonlight and he'd be whispering hoarsely as I struggled: 'That's enough now, Annabelle. Just lie still, be a good girl now and lie still. You're my special little whore and I want to help you. This is going to make you feel better. Lie still and relax. Just relax.'

He was so close to me, so real, I could smell him. It was the sweet smell of stale tobacco on his breath, and I'd want to heave.

At that moment he would sink the needle into my arm and then I'd see Emily appear at the end of the bed, squeezing her toy pterodactyl, looking completely petrified. And the poison would make me go numb, so then he would jump off me and I'd watch helplessly as he went towards my little girl. I'd be screaming and screaming: NO, NO, NO, NO! But I couldn't do anything and now Emily would be crying with fear as he picked her up and I'd be paralysed and desperate. Then I'd see the needle appear again and I would know that this would surely kill her but I wouldn't be able to do a thing about it and I was screaming and screaming but no sound would come out and then . . . and then . . . and then I'd wake up, drenched in sweat, panting and trembling with fear.

The funny thing was I never dreamt about my mum. Never. Not once.

Chapter 23

Moving On

I never expected to fall in love. I suppose I never imagined that it would be possible for me. My life had been so blighted by men that for a very long time I couldn't trust them at all. And once you have worked as a prostitute, it's hard not to feel a warped sense that all men are after just one thing. So, for a very long time, I didn't even think about it. All I wanted to do was concentrate on making a new life for myself and Emily, on moving forward in the best way possible and achieving some kind of stability.

It was hard enough just to manage the basics like going out every day, getting through college, looking after Emily and keeping my finances in order. These are things I'd never had to do on my own before and it was difficult. I'd received compensation after the court case and I made some mistakes with that. I lent money to people and I failed to put in place a plan for repayment. In short, I gave money away which I now know I'll never get back. It was stupid and I was so angry with myself because that was really money I should have set aside for Emily or invested in her future. But I wanted to trust people. I just didn't know how to express that, and I guess I thought that if I gave people money they would honour their promises and return it to me. Yes, I had a lot of growing up to do.

After my first year in college I got a summer job working in a catering firm – we made sandwiches in the morning and sold them to local businesses at lunchtime. It was a fun little job because it was close to my house and there were a few women doing it who all lived near me who were very warm and friendly. They welcomed me into their world and it felt good to have friends again. After I lost touch with Hope, I didn't really have any friends besides my family. The problem was that my family knew everything that had happened to me so, although we all laughed together, there was always a heaviness in the air around us; something dragging at the edges of our hearts.

It was nice to meet people who were normal and fun. They would take the piss out of me, which is something I wasn't used to at first. I was always so terrified of what people thought of me that I was quite guarded around new people. Serious and unsmiling, I wore a full face of make-up every day and didn't really joke around or make small talk with others. But, as time went on, the women at my work made me feel like one of the team and helped me to loosen up a bit.

Maisie was about twenty-five years older than me and a real hoot. We were up very early every morning to prepare the food and then we would go out in the van together, selling our sandwiches and snacks. I loved working with Maisie because she made me howl with laughter. She was the exact opposite of me

— extrovert, bubbly, loud and flamboyant. She always had her nails done in bright colours, wore huge dangly earrings and put her blonde and honey-streaked hair in a giant beehive. With her colourful clothes and towering heels, you couldn't miss her. She made it her personal mission during my first few weeks at work to bring me out of my shell and, I have to confess, she didn't fail!

When Maisie found out I was single she threw her hands up in the air in mock outrage. Then she declared herself the world's greatest matchmaker and announced she would hook me up with someone before the end of the summer.

'It's a sodding crime you being single!' she chided, as she slapped a Kraft cheese slice on a brown roll that morning.

'Why?' I said, taking my time buttering a baguette. 'I don't need a man to make me happy.'

'Darling, nobody *needs* a man!' she scoffed. 'But everyone would like a little bit of attention and fun, honey. All work and no play makes Annabelle a dull girl.'

'Are you calling me dull?'

'Put it this way – I don't class a mug of hot chocolate in front of *EastEnders* an exciting night out. When are you going to come out with me?'

'I've got a little girl, remember.'

'Excuses, excuses. You've also got a built-in babysitting service at your aunt's house.'

'Yeah, well I'm terrified of going out with you, Maisie!' I laughed. 'You'll bury me under a ton of unsuitable men.'

'Exactly, dear Annabelle! Just what you've been missing!' she grinned, holding up her butter knife triumphantly.

I didn't tell Maisie or anyone else at work about my background. It just wasn't that kind of relationship. We had a laugh, we bantered together and that was it. Besides, I didn't need people to feel sorry for me. I didn't want their pity; I just wanted to be accepted for being myself. Having a laugh every day with Maisie made me feel human again. I was connecting with the world outside my home, but this time it was on my terms.

One day, in a quiet moment while we were waiting for customers, she started telling me about her son Finn, who, according to Maisie, was dating the wrong woman.

'Oh, God, she's a nightmare!' Maisie sighed dramatically. 'Honestly, Anna, she gives Finn a really hard time. This weekend they were out and then when they got home they started rowing. It's, like, four in the morning and she's screaming blue murder and it's waking up all their neighbours. In the end, he comes round my house! So I get woken up in the middle of the bloody night to let my twenty-nine-year-old son back home because his girlfriend decides she wants a barney. I keep telling him she's not right for him but, you know, you can't tell them anything. They have to learn for themselves.'

'What's he like, your son?' I was curious.

'Oh, Anna, he'd be just right for you!' she winked playfully.

'I don't mean that!' I laughed. 'You're awful! He's already with someone.'

'Not for much longer,' she said darkly. 'Seriously, I can't see them going the distance. I don't even think he loves her. He's just become wrapped up in all the drama. At some point his eyes will open and he'll see that beyond the fighting there's not an awful lot keeping them together.'

At that moment, Maisie, who had been scrolling down her phone, lifted the screen up to me. There was a handsome blond lad in a checked shirt with his arm around Maisie, smiling warmly at the camera. He had friendly eyes and a very cheeky grin.

'Aw, he looks really nice,' I said appreciatively.

'Yeah, he's a good boy,' she smiled, looking down at her phone now. 'He's got a really good job in an accountancy firm, does well for himself, works hard. You know, last year he bought his own flat. I'm proud of him.'

At that moment she held up her phone again. This time there was a picture of a young boy, around eight years old, riding a bike in a loud orange jumper with floppy hair and that same impish grin. It was clearly Finn as a little boy. I burst out laughing.

'What a cute kid!' I laughed.

'They grow up quickly, my dear!'

I didn't think anything of this at the time but, a week later, Maisie sidled up to me at work, breathless with excitement.

'He saw your picture!' she said, her eyes blazing, her bangles jangling furiously.

'Who? Who did you show my picture to?' I wasn't too happy about this. Maisie had taken some pictures of me for my Facebook page that she had just helped me to set up. But I didn't want her waving the pictures around in front of all her male friends.

'Oh, don't get your knickers in a twist,' she said. 'Just Finn, that's all. We were looking through my phone at the weekend and he came across your picture. He asked me: "Who's that? She's a bit of a sort."'

I blushed then.

'I told him we worked together and he said he thought you looked really nice. Why don't you message him? Look, here's his profile.'

Maisie played around with Facebook on my phone until Finn's page came up. I read all his comments in his timeline and actually started giggling when I read a conversation from the night before.

He'd written: 'Mum, stop reading my Facebook page!'

She'd replied: 'Who is this, please? And why have you dropped your washing at my house?'

'It's all my dirty laundry, Mum. Thought you might be able to keep it to yourself this time instead of giving it a good airing in public. Ooops. Looks like I got that wrong!'

'Ha – he got you there!' I laughed.

'Yeah, well, he's just too sensitive for his own damn good,' she said.

I reflected on this. I liked the fact that Finn wanted to keep his personal business private. I felt the same.

'Go on,' Maisie urged. 'Message him.'

'All right, I will!'

Recalling the picture of the cheeky lad straddling a bike, I messaged Finn: 'You were very cute when you were younger!'

Then I pressed send.

'He's going to break up with her, you know,' Maisie said casually.

'Oh, Maisie!' I exploded.

'What? I'm just *saying*.'

It only took a few minutes before a new message popped into my inbox. I clicked on it: 'Thank you, you're not bad-looking yourself.'

Maisie leaned in and nudged me in the ribs.

'Get your coat, love, I think you've pulled.'

I rolled my eyes at her but inside I was secretly quite pleased and, from then, Finn and I started talking over Facebook.

From the word go, I felt very comfortable with Finn. He was friendly, open and always managed to make me laugh. At first we were just friends online but soon we exchanged phone numbers and we started texting each other. Knowing his mum really helped put me at ease and, though he was still with his girlfriend, I didn't mind because I wasn't looking for a relationship.

At this moment, it was enough that we were just good friends. I'd never been friends with a boy before, I'd never been allowed. Apart from having sex, girls weren't really allowed to mix with boys in the Church, so this was all new territory for me.

Besides, in the early months and years following the court case, I wasn't in a position to have a relationship. I just didn't feel confident of getting together with the right person. Colin had been so dominant I worried I would just look for the same sort of person to fill that void. For now, I needed to stand on my own two feet. I needed to prove to myself that I was capable.

In October 2012, three months after we started talking, I met

Finn for the first time on a night out with his mum and some work colleagues. We hugged like old friends and chatted easily together. He seemed really confident and relaxed and I marvelled at how he took everything in his stride. I was still finding my feet socially and was always so shy in public. At the end of the night, he told me he had split up with his ex-girlfriend.

'I'd really like to go out on a date with you, if that's OK?' he asked hesitantly.

'Erm, well, I'm not sure,' I mumbled. 'Isn't it a bit too soon?'

'I don't think so,' he shrugged. 'I mean, Mum's been right all along about her. I wasn't happy. It just took a long time for me to get out of the relationship.'

'She really looks out for you, you know,' I said.

'Who does?' Finn's face crumpled, perplexed.

'Your mum, silly!' I laughed.

'Oh, yeah,' he smiled. 'Well, it's her job, isn't it? She's my mum!'

I felt a stab of jealousy and annoyance then. Yes, he was right, it was her job. It was just that not all mums loved their jobs or did them as well as Maisie.

'You're lucky, you know,' I said earnestly. 'She's a really lovely woman. Not every mother is like her.'

And we left it at that. I don't know why I said no at first — perhaps I was worried. I really liked Finn and I was afraid of getting intimate. In so many ways, I hadn't had the normal teenage experiences. On the outside I was a 22-year-old mum but inside I felt idiotically young. How would it feel to kiss someone you really liked? I didn't know. Despite my extensive sexual experiences, when it came to love, I was still a real beginner and scared of making mistakes.

Poor boy – in the end I made him wait four months for our first date but that night, 16 February 2013, was perfect. We went out for pizza, talked rubbish for hours and laughed about the stupidest things. As he walked me home that night, he took my hand and it felt so natural and right. I felt my heart beating in my chest, and for all the right reasons. Was this it? Was this the moment he was going to kiss me? Standing at the door, I told him I'd had a brilliant night and he asked if we could do it all again tomorrow night.

'Yeah, all right,' I grinned. He reached up then and gently swept my hair aside from my face.

'You're so beautiful, Anna,' he said simply. 'I like you a lot.'

'I like you too,' I said shyly, barely able to look him in the eyes. 'But . . . well, this is difficult for me.'

'Why? What's difficult?'

'Oh, where do I start? Honestly, Finn, it's long and complicated.'

'I'm not going anywhere,' he said.

There was silence then. I didn't know why, but I felt I had to tell him about my past. If we had any chance of making it work, he had to know the truth. Would he still want to be with me after he found out what I'd done? I hoped so, but I had to know for sure. I couldn't afford to let myself fall in love if he was going to run a mile at the first sign of trouble.

'Let's call it a night, hey?' I suggested quietly. 'Call me in the morning.'

*   *   *

And so it was that on our second date I told Finn everything about my life before. We hadn't even kissed yet and I was laying it all out in front of him – Colin, my mum, Wales. I even directed him to all the articles about the court case online so he could read it for himself. That wasn't easy. I didn't want to do it but I knew it would only get harder if I wasn't honest from the start.

After I'd finished telling him everything, he sat back in the sofa, one palm across his forehead, and a look like he'd just been hit by a ten-ton truck. Then he blew his cheeks out, shook his head with wonder and looked into my eyes.

'You'd never know,' were his first words.

'Never know what?'

'You'd never know you'd been through all that,' he said. 'Anna, how do you do it? You seem so normal! I've known girls who haven't had any trouble in their lives and they're complete screw-ups. You're amazing.'

My eyes filled with tears. I was just so relieved that he hadn't got up and run out the door at that point.

'I'm just trying to get on with my life,' I said, picking at a cushion on my lap. 'It was Emily who saved me. I wouldn't be here today without her. I wanted you to know before anything starts because, well, I don't want to lie to you. It would feel wrong.'

Finn smiled then and took my shaking hands in his: 'You don't have to worry about anything with me. I like you and, as I said, I'm not going anywhere.'

'I want to take things slowly,' I told him.

'That's fine with me. Straight up. Anna, you don't have to do anything you don't want to. I'd never do anything to hurt you.'

And with that he wrapped me in a wonderful bear hug and we stayed like that. There, in his embrace, and for the first time I can ever remember, I felt safe. And happy.

Finn and I may have started slowly but, once we'd got over that first hurdle of establishing trust, there was no stopping us. Kissing Finn was a revelation. It was amazing! I just wanted to kiss him for ages and ages but I guess things tend to progress naturally and, by July, I had moved into his place. A month later, I found out I was pregnant. Initially we were both really shocked and I wondered if we were moving too quickly. It was Finn in the end that persuaded me it was a blessing.

'Look, we both love each other,' he said. 'This would have happened a few years down the line anyway. It feels right to me and if it feels right to you too, then who's to say if it is too quick? I was with someone for years and it was all wrong. I waited long enough to find you. I don't want to waste any more time starting a family together!'

I didn't need any more persuading. I knew Finn would make a great dad – already him and Emily were brilliant friends and, finally, I felt I'd found the stability I'd been searching for all this time. With Finn, Maisie and the new baby, I felt I was putting down roots and creating a little space for myself in this life. A little world that felt good, happy and wholesome.

Epilogue

In February this year, 2014, our little family was complete when I gave birth to my gorgeous son – Finn Junior. Now Emily is seven and loving being a big sister to her baby brother. As for me, I'm making the most of every moment, enjoying all the early weeks of motherhood without the stress and fear that I had with Emily when I lived in Wales. I feel like I can truly be the mother I want to be, right from the very start.

That's not to say it has all been plain sailing. I am still haunted by nightmares, I still hear Colin's voice in my head sometimes and I can still feel overwhelmed by the outside world. There are days I want to hide myself away and not see anyone. There are times I can't make a decision, even about the smallest things, and I tend to defer to Finn. But he doesn't always let me do this – he's determined I should find my own voice and make my own decisions, however painful it is for me to do that.

He doesn't ask too many questions about the past – I know it pains him to think about it so we don't talk about the things I have done or that have been done to me.

'You were forced to do those things, Anna,' he says. 'If I ever saw that man so help me I'd kill him.'

It's hard to explain to him how complicated my feelings are towards Colin. He doesn't understand why I don't hate him too – I struggle to make sense of it all myself.

And there are times I just don't want to talk. There are times when I become very shut off from the world and I close down to him. He has to try very hard to get me back again because it's almost like I disappear into myself. On the outside, I'll be silent and still – you wouldn't guess the tumult I'm feeling within.

One thing I've had to learn from scratch is showing emotion to him. Apart from with Emily, I'm usually very unwilling to show my emotions to anyone. In the past it has been a weakness used against me in a war of manipulation. I learned how to put on a mask and hide behind it.

That drives Finn crazy.

'You don't have to hide yourself away!' he tells me. 'Emotion isn't a weakness. Not everyone will take advantage of you. If you feel like having a cry – that's fine. Have a cry! If you're angry with me, tell me. I can't be in a relationship with someone who is always hiding.'

Occasionally I am rocked by an unexpected jolt of loneliness when I see Finn and his mum joking around together. They're so close. But they're sensitive too and always include me in everything. Maisie and I have our own special relationship too. She's nutty as a fruitcake and I love her to death! After all, I have her to thank for my happiness. When I hear Finn talking to his mum disrespectfully it makes me so mad. I want to shake him and tell him how lucky he is to have her. I do wish I had a mum like her. Getting used to life without one is hard, very hard.

I haven't contacted my dad since I came back to London. I don't know why – I guess I'm hoping that one day he'll get in touch with me. I don't hold any grudges or anger towards him – I understand that none of it was his fault. I just hope that one day he might choose to invite me into his life. That would be very nice.

I miss my brother and sister. I see Olivia from time to time but she has her own life now – she is out of care and she has a boy-friend. She's eighteen and I know one day I'll have to have the talk with her about Mum and Colin. I will wait until she is ready. Until then, I hope she knows I am always there for her, just as Finn is always there for me.

I still get angry. It amazes me, even to this day, that there were so many people who came into contact with us 'Church' children who never saw anything to give them cause for alarm. We lived in a cul-de-sac with lots of other houses – the neigh-bours never saw or heard anything either. Even the people who had left the cult were too frightened to tell the truth to the authorities. In the end, we suffered because everyone else looked away.

Today, I try to be the best mum I can. And despite everything I have been through, I consider myself lucky. Lucky to have a healthy son and a happy, healthy seven-year-old daughter. Emily makes me laugh every day – the way she bounds in from school, eager to show me her latest drawings or gets excited when we find a new dinosaur book. I love the way she throws her arms around me when she's upset, like she never wants to let me go, or even the way she pokes her tongue out at me when she's having a strop. And I know now that she doesn't just have me – she has all these other people in her life too. People who care and love her and will never let her fall. I look in her eyes and I see all that strength and life and I know I will never ever, ever let her down.

I will never look away.

Information and Support

Colin Batley's cult was based on Aleister Crowley's early twentieth-century text, *The Book of The Law*, whose guiding principle can be summarized by the single sentence: 'Do what thou wilt.' Crowley was an occultist, ceremonial magician, poet and mountaineer and founded the religion and philosophy of Thelema. Crowley's libertine lifestyle as an openly bisexual drug user and social critic led the press to denounce him at the time as 'the wickedest man in the world'.

According to Crowley, his *Book of The Law* was based on a vision during which he was told that humanity was entering a new era and he was to serve as its prophet, spreading the philosophy that humans should basically seek to follow their own path, no matter what. Worship in his cult was formed of sadomasochistic sex rituals with both sexes, spells to raise the Malevolent Gods and the use of hard drugs.

Crowley's philosophy was used by Batley to control and dominate others, to get them to satisfy his twisted sexual whims and transgress their moral boundaries. Innocent children were harmed. The judge in the case against Batley and his harem described Crowley's text as a 'clearly ridiculous document'.

Various celebrities have endorsed the order that Crowley founded called the Ordo Templi Orientis, known as OTO, though few make the connection between Crowley and his perverted modern-day followers like Batley.

Further reading/Support

CIC – Cult Information Centre
Web: cultinformation.org.uk
Tel: 0845 4500 868
The CIC is a charity providing advice and information for victims of cults, their families and friends, researchers and the media.

NAPAC – The National Association for People Abused in
    Childhood
Web: napac.org.uk
Tel: 0800 085 3330
A registered charity, based in the UK, providing support and information for people abused in childhood.

ChildLine
Web: childline.org.uk
Tel: 0800 1111
ChildLine is a private and confidential service for children and young people up to the age of nineteen. You can contact a

ChildLine counsellor about anything – no problem is too big or too small. Calls are free.

NSPCC

Web: nspcc.org.uk

Tel: 0808 800 5000

The National Society for the Prevention of Cruelty to Children protects children across the UK. They run a wide range of services for both children and adults, including national helplines and local projects. Worried about a child? Don't wait until you're certain. Contact the NSPCC's trained helpline counsellors for 24/7 help, advice and support.

Samaritans

Web: samaritans.org

Tel: 08457 90 90 90

If there's something that's troubling you it can be a tremendous help to talk to someone who isn't a family member or a friend. You don't have to be suicidal to get in touch. Available 24 hours a day, 365 days a year.